DECEPTION DELUSION & DESTRUCTION

By Dave Williams

MOUNT HOPE BOOKS
A Division of Decapolis Publishing House
202 South Creyts Rd. • Lansing, MI 48917

Unless otherwise indicated, all Scripture quotations are taken from the *Authorized King James Version* of the Bible.

Edited by Phil Bowden
Illustrations by Tim Drier
Dave Williams' Photos by Marvin Hall

ISBN-0-938020-43-9
Copyright © 1991 David R. Williams

Published by Mount Hope Books
A Division of Decapolis Publishing House
202 South Creyts Road
Lansing, Michigan 48917

Printed in the United States of America. All rights reserved under International Copyright Law. Contents and/or cover may not be reproduced in whole or in part in any form without the express written consent of the Publisher.

CONTENTS

Chapter One: Deception 1

Chapter Two: What is Deception? 5

Chapter Three: Who are Targets for
    Deception? 9

Chapter Four: Compromising
    Christians 15

Chapter Five: More Targets for
    Deception 25

Chapter Six: Who is the Master-Mind
    Behind Deception? 37

Chapter Seven: Religious Deception 49

Chapter Eight: Danger Signs 63

Chapter Nine: More Targets for
    Deception 77

Chapter Ten: Who Tends to Follow
    the False? 85

Chapter Eleven: On the Thin Edge
    of Disaster 95

Chapter Twelve: Our Divine Defense
    Against Deception 103

DECEPTION DELUSION & DESTRUCTION

Ye are of God, little children, and have overcome them: because greater is He that is in you, than he that is in the world.
— I John 4:4

Chapter One: Deception!

How does he do it? I watched in disbelief and outright bewilderment. There he was appearing on my television screen, blowing smoke from his Cuban cigar, swearing at me, making lewd remarks, singing filthy songs to God, talking about his "Jesus" and why I need to send in my money now. Imagine that! I watched, flabbergasted, as the man raised millions of dollars from undiscerning viewers calling in their pledges, claiming to have cashed in their retirement accounts, sold homes, and closed bank accounts in order to send this smoke-blowing, cussing, "preacher" their money for his "God-anointed project."

Deception.

It happened again. I'll never forget that shocking November night in 1978. The news media screamed on all corners, "900 CULT MEMBERS DEAD." Shock waves pulsated around the world when "Reverend" Jim Jones and 912 deluded followers were thrust into eternity in a massive cult suicide/murder pact. Jim Jones, a communist, masquerading as a minister of religion, led hundreds astray. Many sincere people died that night, leaving their loved ones to "pick up the pieces."

> For such are false apostles, deceitful workers, transforming themselves into the apostles of Christ. And no marvel; for Satan himself is transformed into an angel of light. Therefore it is no great thing if his ministers also be transformed as the ministers of righteousness; whose end shall be according to their works.
> — II Corinthians 11:13-15

Deception!

Jesus sternly warned us about deception. In fact He said the primary sign of His Return would be the increase in worldwide deception. Look at his first answer in every account where the disciples asked for a sign of His Coming:

> And Jesus answered and said unto them, Take heed that no man deceive you. For many shall come in my name, saying, I am Christ; and shall deceive many.
> — Matthew 24:4-5

> And Jesus answering them began to say, Take heed lest any man deceive you: For many shall come in my name, saying, I am Christ; and shall deceive many.
> — Mark 13:5-6

> And He said, Take heed that ye be not deceived: for many shall come in my name, saying, I am

Deception!

> Christ; and the time draweth near: go ye not therefore after them.
>
> — Luke 21:8

At this moment, a cloud of confusion covers our world. It blankets the economy, the political world, the religious world . . . everywhere. Things are becoming increasingly complicated. We are involved in a warfare — a spiritual warfare employing espionage, agents, counter agents, impersonators, and impostors. (Acts 20:28-30)

The modern world is rapidly being prepared for the appearance of the supreme deception of this age — the long-awaited, dreaded Antichrist!

> Even him whose coming is after the working of Satan with all power and signs and lying wonders, And with all deceivableness of unrighteousness in them that perish; because they received not the love of the truth, that they might be saved.
>
> — II Thessalonians 2:9-10

I have some bad news for you. Deception is going to get worse, not better, in the days just ahead.

> But evil men and seducers shall wax WORSE and WORSE, deceiving, and being deceived.
>
> — II Timothy 3:13

Now I have some good news for you. The Bible gives us clear guidelines on how to recognize deception, enlightening us on how to keep free from all forms of this subtle spiritual blindness. In this book, I'll define deception, expose the common targets for deception, and reveal how you can recognize the most deadly form of deception of all — religious deception.

Deception, Delusion & Destruction

Let's first take a look at what deception really is....

Remember . . .

☑ 1. Jesus warned us about deception.

☑ 2. The primary sign of Christ's return will be the increase in deception.

☑ 3. Like it or not, you are involved in a spiritual warfare.

☑ 4. Deception is going to get worse in the days ahead.

☑ 5. The Bible, God's Word, gives us clear guidelines which, when followed, will keep us free from deception.

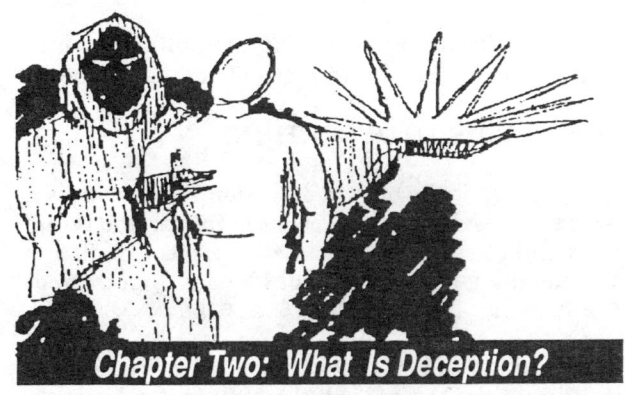

Chapter Two: What Is Deception?

What is deception?

Deception is defined from the Greek language as "roaming or wandering; erring, or being seduced, or deluded." Deception is always an undercover strategy of the enemy. The victim does not realize he's been a target. Like a good bear trap, deception is hidden, to be realized only after it's too late; after its victim has been lured and helplessly and torturously snared.

There are no identification flags flying above the land mines of deception. Traps are hidden, secret, unseen. This is what makes deception triply dangerous.

The person drifting into deception doesn't fully recognize the lure. He may sense that something is amiss, but for a variety of reasons, will likely deny it. Others may see him wandering into deception, and confront him, but quickly, he will assure them that everything is fine. Like a drug addict, or an alcoholic, he will deny the lure of deception that's pulling him into an "off-limits" area — a "forbidden fruit," so-to-speak.

WHAT LEADS TO DECEPTION?

What opens the door to deception? What causes a person to wander or to be seduced into tragic error? Many things could lead to deception, but I've discovered one thing in particular that is usually at the root of it. And that is simply this: SELF-WILL.

Deception seems to begin in the heart as a result of honoring one's personal will above the will of Almighty God. Let me restate that for emphasis. DECEPTION BEGINS IN THE HEART THE MOMENT A PERSON HONORS HIS PERSONAL WILL ABOVE THE WILL OF ALMIGHTY GOD!

In the newspaper I read recently of a teenager who was found lying dead at the side of his house. He had committed suicide after butchering his loving family to death. What caused this young man to "snap"? According to the news report, he had recently started listening to a satanic rock and roll group and had attended one of their Satan-honoring concerts. His parents tried to reason with him, objecting to his music preference and protesting his attendance of the concert. But it was too late. He honored his own will instead, became quickly deceived, and violently lost control to outside forces of darkness.

> For we are not fighting against people made of flesh and blood, but against persons without bodies — the evil rulers of the unseen world, those mighty satanic beings and great evil princes of darkness who rule this world; and against huge numbers of wicked spirits in the spirit world.
> — Ephesians 6:12 (TLB)

What Is Deception?

Deceived. Lost. Right now he sits in the lower regions of the damned, awaiting his fearful and eternal judgment.

> And I saw a great white throne, and Him that sat on it, from whose face the earth and the heaven fled away; and there was found no place for them. And I saw the dead, small and great, stand before God; and the books were opened: and another book was opened, which is the book of life: and the dead were judged out of those things which were written in the books, according to their works.
> — Revelation 20:11-12

Please understand, I'm not suggesting that everyone who listens to satanic music becomes instantly deceived and possessed by demonic creatures. But it can happen. And it can happen quickly.

I remember receiving an emergency call from the hospital one day. A young man who once attended our church had sliced his wrists with a razor blade, then shoved straightened coat hangers into his bleeding veins. After the initial shock, I discovered this fellow had, three months prior, begun to honor his own personal will above the will of Almighty God. How? He began engaging in homosexual activities with his landlord.

Deceived!

If you have been following self-will instead of God's will, and you realize it, there is hope for you. Jesus still sets the captives free. And that includes those who are captive to self-will. I'll share more in later chapters about Christ's delivering power.

Deception, Delusion & Destruction

Where does deception begin? It begins in the heart, when we honor our personal will over God's perfect will.

In the next chapter we'll take a look at some classes of people who are prime candidates for deception.

Remember ...

- ☑ 1. Deception is an undercover work which causes its victim to roam or wander slowly away.

- ☑ 2. The chief tool that invites deception is self-will.

- ☑ 3. Deception begins in the heart when we honor our own will over God's perfect will.

Chapter Three:
Who are the Targets for Deception?

Are there certain classes of people who become easy targets for Satan's deceptions? The answer is YES! The Bible offers clear insight into this matter.

TARGETS FOR DECEPTION

☑ 1. *Those who are not born again.* These people may be church members. They may not be.

Jesus said, "Verily, verily," (Note: Whenever the Bible says "verily, verily," it means a fundamental, critical truth is about to be expressed.) "I say unto thee, Except a man be born again, he cannot see the kingdom of God." (John 3:3)

Jesus was speaking of a spiritual rebirth that comes to us when we, by an act of choice, turn from our sins and turn toward God by receiving Jesus Christ, who died on the cross, as our only hope of being saved. We do this by calling out to God in repentance of our sin, believing in our hearts that God raised Jesus from the dead, and that He will, by His Spirit, come and abide in our lives giving us a new birth; a spiritual

Deception, Delusion & Destruction

birth. (Romans 10:9; Acts 2:38, 39; John 14:16,17) You don't have to understand it, only believe it.

The words of Jesus in John 3:3 are interesting as it relates to deception. Let's look at them again.

> Verily, verily, I say unto thee, Except a man be born again HE CANNOT SEE the Kingdom of God.

He CANNOT SEE. He is blind spiritually. Deceived. Blindness, in figurative Biblical language, means deceived. Those who haven't deliberately turned their lives over to Jesus Christ CANNOT SEE: They are essentially deceived.

> Having the understanding darkened, being alienated from the life of God through the ignorance that is in them, because of the blindness of their heart.
> — Ephesians 4:18

> But their minds were blinded...
> — II Corinthians 3:14a

That blindness, however, can be driven out. The moment a person believes on Jesus Christ and receives Him into his life by faith, deception begins to break. Suddenly he can SEE. You've heard the expression, "I saw the light." That's not a bad expression. "I SAW."

The familiar hymn, AMAZING GRACE, says it beautifully.

> I once was lost,
> But now am found;
> Was blind,
> But now I SEE!

Those who are not born again, have their minds blinded (deceived) by the god (little "g" — god; Satan) of this world.

Who are the Targets for Deception?

> But if our gospel be hid, it is hid to them that are lost: In whom the god of this world hath blinded the minds of them which believe not, lest the light of the glorious gospel of Christ, who is the image of God, should shine unto them.
> — II Corinthians 4:3-4

They have no revelation and no way of uncovering the hidden traps of growing darkness and deeper deception. They are bound for eternal hell, but don't know it because of DECEPTION.

Some are deceived into thinking mere morality will give them entrance into heaven. Others are deceived into believing there is no real hell. Prominent false teachers of our generation promote the "no hell" concept, and literally millions have followed their lures and swallowed their hooks of deception.

The one who has never committed his life to Christ will find the Bible to be dry and boring. That's because there's no revelation; no Holy Spirit to enlighten the sacred truths to him.

> Thy Word is a lamp unto my feet, and a light unto my path.
> — Psalm 119:105

So they wander on, believing anything they choose, listening week-after-week to men in pulpits who themselves have no spiritual life.

A clear eighty percent of all cult members were originally members of nominal Christian churches. But were they ever born again? It's not likely.

> Howbeit when he, the Spirit of truth, is come, he will guide you into all truth: for he shall not speak

Deception, Delusion & Destruction

> of himself; but whatsoever he shall hear, that shall he speak: and he will shew you things to come. He shall glorify me: for he shall receive of mine, and shall shew it unto you.
> — John 16:13-14

He (the Holy Spirit) SHOWS US things of importance that God wants us to know. He gives us spiritual eyes. Only the born-again person can see spiritual truths. Only the born-again person can be assured of a home in heaven when death calls or Jesus returns.

It's amazing what the blinded mind can believe. Reincarnation. No hell. Mediators other than Jesus. Animal worship. False concepts about eternal life. Flying saucers will save us. Astrology. ESP. The list could go on to fill a fifteen thousand volume set of hardcover books! Yet not one of these beliefs came from the Bible or from God, the Author.

So, the first class of people who are candidates for deception, and indeed are already walking in a form of deception, is those who have not committed their lives to Christ; those who have never experienced being "born again." When death finally calls, they will be in for the greatest real-life horror they ever imagined.

Are you born again? Do you want to avoid deception? If I were you, I'd find a good church where the Number One belief is that the Bible is God's infallible Word. Ask someone there to pray with you. They'll be glad to help you become born again.

But why wait? You can have this experience right where you are now. Ask Jesus to enter your heart. He will. And you'll be born again. Then, tell someone what you did. That's important.

Who are the Targets for Deception

That if thou shalt confess with thy mouth the Lord Jesus, and shalt believe in thine heart that God hath raised Him form the dead, thou shalt be saved.
— Romans 10:9

In the next chapter we'll hit closer to home with you who are already born again.

Remember ...

☑ 1. Church members who are not born again are great candidates for deception.

☑ 2. Only by turning from sin and to God, through Jesus Christ, can we be "born again."

☑ 3. The unsaved church member is spiritually blind.

☑ 4. Eighty percent of all cult members were once members of nominal churches.

☑ 5. Church members who aren't born again have only the terrors of eternal hell to look forward to, regardless of how good they've been.

Chapter Four: Compromising Christians

In the last days, just before Christ's coming, some believers will depart from the faith, giving heed to seducing spirits and doctrines of demons.

> Now the Spirit speaketh expressly, that in the latter times some shall depart from the faith, giving heed to seducing spirits, and doctrines of devils."
> — I Timothy 4:1

Departing from the faith. The structure of this phrase in I Timothy is such that it implies the possibility of drifting away from authentic faith in Christ. True Christianity, in the early days, was called "the faith." It is possible for Christians to drift, wander, and err from the faith. You see, you can only depart from someplace you've been. You can't depart from Detroit if you aren't already in Detroit. You cannot depart from "the faith" if you're not already in "the faith."

How does this departure occur? It happens through seducing spirits or false doctrines. It's DECEPTION. Slow. Subtle. Effective.

Deception, Delusion & Destruction

Let's look at some classes of Christians who have opened the door to deception, allowing it to slither into their lives.

THE FIRST CHRISTIAN CANDIDATES FOR DECEPTION ARE:

☑ 1. *Those who hear but do not obey the Word of God.*

> Be ye DOERS of the Word, and not hearers only, deceiving your own selves.
> — James 1:22

> Not every one that saith unto me, Lord, Lord, shall enter into the kingdom of heaven; but he that DOETH the will of my Father which is in heaven.
> — Matthew 7:21

These folks are self-deceived. Why should the devil spend time trying to deceive this type of Christian? They've done a pretty good job of it themselves.

A SECOND CLASS OF THOSE ON THE ROAD TO DECEPTION IS:

☑ 2. *Christians with licentious attitudes.* They call it "Christian liberty," but the truth is, they've used their liberty as an excuse to sin.

> While they promise them liberty, they themselves are the servants of corruption: for of whom a man is overcome, of the same is he brought in bondage.
> — II Peter 2:19

True Christian liberty is *liberty from sin*, deception, oppression, and bondage; NOT liberty *to* sin.

Compromising Christians

> Know ye not that the unrighteous shall not inherit the kingdom of God? BE NOT DECEIVED: neither fornicators, nor idolaters nor adulterers, nor effeminate, nor abusers of themselves with mankind, nor thieves, nor covetous, nor drunkards, nor revilers, nor extortioners, shall inherit the kingdom of God.
>
> —I Corinthians 6:9-10

Now notice the next verse:

> And such WERE (past tense) some of you: but ye are washed, but ye are sanctified, but ye are justified in the name of the Lord Jesus, and by the Spirit of our God.
>
> —I Corinthians 6:11 (parenthesis mine)

I read this verse one Sunday evening in church. There were about a thousand people in attendance, *former* drug addicts, *former* prostitutes, *former* adulterers, and *former* homosexuals. But some were present who were still practicing these sins, loving them, and had no mind to change their ways. They were making excuses for their sins, justifying themselves; distorting the reality of God's Word.

"BE NOT DECEIVED." The words could be no clearer or more precise. "BE NOT DECEIVED." God gives no believer a license to sin; He gives the believer liberty from sin, to serve God in newness of life and holiness.

> But if, while we seek to be justified by Christ, we ourselves also are found sinners, is therefore Christ the minister of sin? God forbid.
>
> —Galatians 2:17

Deception, Delusion & Destruction

> For brethren, ye have been called unto liberty; only use not liberty for an occasion to the flesh, but by love serve one another.
> — Galatians 5:13

Now, let me be quick to add that sometimes Christians *are deceived* into sins and habits, and even addictions that are harmful to themselves. Some of them live tortured lives, no longer in control.

To these people, I would say this: If you recognize your habit or addiction, whether it be tobacco, gambling, pornography, alcohol, or whatever, as a sin against God, and you are willing to look to God as your Friend and Ally, not your enemy, He will help you obtain deliverance.

> Ye are of God, little children, and have overcome them: because greater is he that is in you, than he that is in the world.
> — I John 4:4

> For sin shall not have dominion over you: for ye are not under the law, but under grace.
> — Romans 6:14

God loves mankind. He loves His Church. We are His precious children and, just as a father would help his child who was playing with something potentially dangerous, so God will help YOU!

God's love for you hasn't changed just because you were deceived into a practice that now masters you. He wants you out. But do you want out?

If so, admit that you are powerless to break this sin. Believe God is able and willing to help you. Turn

Compromising Christians

yourself completely over to His loving care to do whatever is necessary. Confess specifically each incidence of failure. Ask for God's assistance and look to another Christian for help and accountability. You can't conquer sins by yourself, but with God, and God's family, you'll get your miracle.

BUT . . . to those who are making excuses:

"I've been working hard lately . . . I deserve a drink now and then."

"My wife's mad at me . . . I deserve to look at pornography."

"I need some money . . . there's nothing wrong with buying a lottery ticket or two."

"God understands . . . I have a stronger urge than most men."

Baloney! You're living a double life. You're a phoney, a hypocrite. You've taken the name of the Lord (CHRIST-ian) in vain.

But it's not too late if you see the deception and decide to GET OUT NOW. God will help you.

ANOTHER TYPE OF DECEPTION-BOUND BELIEVERS:

☑ 3. *Those who refuse to believe the law of sowing and reaping.*

Be not deceived; God is not mocked: for whatsoever a man soweth, that shall he also reap.
— Galatians 6:7

Deception, Delusion & Destruction

The Bible is packed with examples of this law, or principle.

Sow criticism toward another, and it'll come back to you.

> Judge not, that ye be not judged. For with what judgment ye judge, ye shall be judged: and with what measure ye mete, it shall be measured to you again.
> — Matthew 7:1-2

Sow mercy to another, and mercy will come back to you.

> Be ye therefore merciful, as your Father also is merciful. Judge not, and ye shall not be judged: condemn not, and ye shall not be condemned: forgive, and ye shall be forgiven: Give, and it shall be given unto you; good measure, pressed down, and shaken together, and running over, shall men give into your bosom. For with the same measure that ye mete withal it shall be measured unto you again.
> — Luke 6:36-38

Sow to the flesh, and you'll reap corruption. Sow to the Spirit, and you'll reap life everlasting.

> Be not deceived; God is not mocked: for whatsoever a man soweth, that shall he also reap. For he that soweth to his flesh shall reap corruption; but he that soweth to the Spirit shall of the Spirit reap life everlasting.
> — Galatians 6:7-8

Sow money into God's work, and you'll reap financial gain in this life.

Compromising Christians

> But this I say, He which soweth sparingly shall reap also sparingly; and he which soweth bountifully shall reap also bountifully. Every man according as he purposeth in his heart, so let him give; not grudgingly, or of necessity: for God loveth a cheerful giver.
>
> — II Corinthians 9:6-7

I don't have the space to go into all the intricate details about sowing and reaping, but in a nutshell, it's this: Whatever you plant will grow and return a yield of like kind. For instance, plant one kernel of corn and you'll receive a whole stalk of corn.

Those who don't believe the principle of sowing and reaping will fall prey to some form of deception, missing God's best for their lives!

Do you need healing? Then pray for the sick. This is planting a seed for your healing.

Do you need money? Then plant a seed of money into God's work. There are literally dozens of promises in God's Word for a good return on your investment into His work.

Do you need mercy because of some foolish thing you've done? Are you in trouble? Then plant a seed of mercy into someone else's life who is struggling.

I know a minister who was consistently harsh and critical of other ministries and would lambast them for their every noticeable fault. He could have chosen to be merciful, instead he chose to be judgmental.

Then it was his turn to fall into serious fault. He wanted mercy. Instead a thousand calls a day flooded

Deception, Delusion & Destruction

his overseer's office, demanding harsh penalties. Even his followers cried out for strict punishment for this man.

The same chapter in Galatians that speaks of sowing and reaping begins with this verse:

> Brethren, if a man be overtaken in a fault, ye which are spiritual, restore such an one in the spirit of meekness; considering thyself, lest thou also be tempted.
> — Galatians 6:1

The amazing law of sowing and reaping. It's unchangeable. Instead of fighting it, side-stepping it, and trying to ignore it, why not get in harmony with it?

Elmer Wheeler, a super salesman was chatting with Bill Patterson, then president of United Airlines and said, "Bill, it's wonderful how we've conquered the air."

Bill replied, "We didn't conquer the air, Elmer. We just got in harmony with the laws that were there all along."

Don't try to conquer the law of sowing and reaping. Just get in harmony with it if you wish to avoid deception.

Now we've looked at three classes of compromising Christians who are easy objects for Satan's deceptions. In the next chapter, we'll discuss other classes who are easy prey for the dreadful land mines of the enemy's deceit.

Compromising Christians

Remember ...

☑ 1. It is possible to depart from the faith; to leave the pathway to heaven for the highway to hell.

☑ 2. The first three classes of Christians who are easy candidates for the terrors of deception are:

   a) Those who hear but do not obey God's Word.
   b) Those with licentious attitudes.
   c) Those who disbelieve the law of sowing and reaping.

Chapter Five:
More Targets for Deception

In chapter four we looked at the first three classes of easily deceived Christians.

☑ 1. *Those who hear, but do not obey God's Word.*

☑ 2. *Christians with licentious attitudes.*

☑ 3. *Those who disbelieve the law of sowing and reaping.*

LET'S TAKE A LOOK AT MORE:

☑ 4. *Those who have an improper concept of riches are candidates for deception.*

He also that received seed among the thorns is he that heareth the Word; and the care of this world, and the DECEITFULNESS of riches, choke the Word, and he becometh unfruitful.

— Matthew 13:22

25

Deception, Delusion & Destruction

How many sincere Christians do you know who have pursued the path to riches, only to grow farther from God's plan for them? I know dozens.

One day a rich young leader came to Jesus, asking Him what he must do to inherit eternal life. He told Jesus that he had kept all of God's moral laws since his childhood.

Jesus responded to the young man with an unusual reply.

"There's one thing you lack. Go sell all your possessions and give the money to the poor. Then come, take up your cross and follow me."

The young man was grieved for he had many possessions (See Mark 10:17-22).

Many preachers have wrongly interpreted this passage of Scripture. They teach that Jesus held a scorn for men's riches. But that's simply not true. Jesus was not against riches at all. In fact, He showed us the pathway to true riches including financial wealth. He taught more about money than He did about heaven or hell.

What He wanted was Lordship. That's all. Obedience. He wanted the young man to seek God's Kingdom, as a priority, then the riches would be returned in a multiplied form, and the young man's priorities would have been straight. The key: Obey Jesus. Follow Jesus. Then, you can have riches and eternal life too! (Mark 10:29-30)

But many have an improper concept of riches. As

More Targets for Deception

a result, they become deceived and miss God's best for their lives.

Some live below God's intended standards for their lives. Others try to live beyond their God-given means. Both are deceived.

As Christians, obedience is our keynote. Jesus said, "If you love me, obey me." (John 14:15)

A simple fundamental law for obtaining riches is this:

> But seek ye first the kingdom of God, and His righteousness; and all these THINGS shall be added unto you.
>
> — Matthew 6:33

God wants His children to have things. Read Matthew 6 again. Then read it again. Ask the Holy Spirit to reveal to your heart the truths of this principle.

To be quite frank, I've never seen a Christian maintain his love relationship with God while directly pursuing riches. I'm amazed at the great number of Christians who become sidetracked into "get rich quick" schemes. I see it all too often. Then when the riches don't materialize as they had hoped, they believe God let them down.

Greediness has no place in the heart of the believer. Greed deceives. But so does the concept of "poverty equals godliness." There are two extremes: "Riches means God's favor" and "Poverty brings God's favor." Both are deceptions.

Get a Bible-concept of riches and wealth. Go to God's Word. He's promised to give you the *power* to get wealth.

Deception, Delusion & Destruction

> But thou shalt remember the Lord thy God: for it is He that giveth thee power to get wealth, that He may establish His covenant which He sware unto thy fathers, as it is this day.
>
> — Deuteronomy 8:18

Remember this: It's God who gives you the power to get wealth. Seek God *FIRST*. Don't be like the deceived believers who drop out of church in order to educate themselves to get a better job so they can have more money. Without God's favor and power, you can attain a Ph.D. and still be on public assistance. In fact, I know of some right now who are.

Next...

☑ 5. *Those believers who fail in character development are on the path to deeper deception.*

> Whereby are given unto us exceeding great and precious promises: that by these ye might be partakers of the divine nature, having escaped the corruption that is in the world through lust. And beside this, giving all diligence, add to your faith virtue; and to virtue, knowledge; and to knowledge, temperance; and to temperance, patience; and to patience, godliness; and to godliness, brotherly kindness; and to brotherly kindness, charity. For if these things be in you, and abound, they make you that ye shall neither be barren nor unfruitful in the knowledge of our Lord Jesus Christ. But he that lacketh these things IS BLIND (deceived), and cannot see afar off, and hath forgotten that he was purged from his old sins.
>
> — II Peter 1:4-9

One day, at the judgement seat of Christ, we will be judged by our character. But most people go through

More Targets for Deception

life without a genuine, serious commitment to character development.

Peter says the person is blind (deceived) who forgets to add to his faith these other great attributes.

What is the difference between character and personality? Dr. Frank Houston, a prominent minister from Sydney, Australia sums it up this way:

> Personality is what other people think you are. Character is what God knows you are.

Character is discerning between right and wrong, and then forcing yourself to choose what's right. Jesus concentrated on teaching character attributes. You see, our character will dictate how we behave in life.

History is laced with men who conquered their worlds, but couldn't conquer their character, thus ended in disaster. Alexander the Great captured the world, but couldn't conquer his character. He wound up killing his best friend in a drunken rage, and dying himself at the young age of thirty-three.

St. Peter gives us a clear pathway for character development. When we follow that path, we are free from what I call "character deception." When we stray from this path, however, we become targets for strong deception and delusion in others areas.

We are saved by grace through FAITH in Christ's accomplished work on the cross. That's simple. But it's just the beginning. Now there's a new road to actively travel if we wish to prevent the disaster of deception. It's the road called "Character Development."

Deception, Delusion & Destruction

Incidentally, deception will always lead your life backwards, from joy to gloominess, from genuine prosperity to poverty, form victory to defeat. The journey downward is not likely an instant process, but a slow, day-by-day, gradual slide downward.

Peter reminds us that we are to ADD to our faith these important character attributes:

a) VIRTUE
b) KNOWLEDGE
c) TEMPERANCE
d) PATIENCE
e) GODLINESS
f) BROTHERLY KINDNESS
g) CHARITY

Do you know someone who radiates with the love of Jesus; he sees the good in people and always seeks to help others through their struggles? That someone has undoubtedly walked the pathway of character development.

Character. Some folks have charisma, but no character. Samson had charisma, but lacked character. His enemies gouged his eyes out and made a slave of him. This is the fate of those who fail in walking the path of character development: Blindness. Deception. Bondage.

It's interesting when the Bible talks about false prophets and false brethren, it always refers to their character, more than their ministries or their work "for God." Read II Peter chapter two to learn the character of false believers and false prophets. It's amazing that

More Targets for Deception

Peter would expose the character of the false believers right after the chapter on how to develop in true Christian character.

Allow Jesus Christ to work deep in your heart today to develop a solid depth of genuine character. Walk the path of character development. If you do, you'll avoid the snare of "character deception."

☑ 6. *Those who hate others are deceived.*

Those who harbor unforgiveness or resentment are targets for deception. These attitudes are forms of hatred. And that hatred produces darkness — DECEPTION.

> He that loveth his brother abideth in the light, and there is none occasion of stumbling in him. But he that hateth his brother is in darkness, and walketh in darkness, and knoweth not whither he goeth, because that darkness has blinded his eyes.
> — I John 2:10-11

> He that hateth dissembleth with his lips, and layeth up deceit within him.
> — Proverbs 26:24

THE NEXT CLASS OF BELIEVER WHO IS RACING TOWARD DECEPTION IS:

☑ 7. *The believer living in careless ease.*

> And take heed to yourselves, lest at any time your hearts be over-charged with surfeiting, and drunkenness, and cares of this life, and so that day come upon you unawares. For as a snare shall it come on all them that dwell on the face of the whole earth.
> — Luke 21:34-35

Deception, Delusion & Destruction

Some professing Christians, in the end times, will have unsuspectingly departed from the faith through deception. Don't let this be you.

These people become possessed with thoughts of pleasure, and activities catering to the senses. Their concern slowly shifts from things of eternal value to things of the temporal.

One day when Jesus comes, they'll be shocked to discover they've been left behind, deceived by their careless ease.

✓ 8. *Those who drink alcohol.*

> Wine is a mocker, strong drink is raging: and whosoever is DECEIVED thereby is not wise.
> — Proverbs 20:1

I am amazed and disgusted with the number of professing Christians who believe that social drinking is acceptable. Acceptable? Yes, for those who are deceived.

I've heard every excuse to support such misconduct. "Well, Jesus turned the water to wine." "Paul told Timothy to drink some wine for his stomach's sake." I think I've heard them all. And there's no point in telling these deceived individuals that the alcohol content in Biblical wine (like the disciples drank) was less than one percent alcohol. Today's wine is twelve to fourteen percent alcohol. They'll fight, they'll argue, they'll justify their deplorable practice, and then try to use God's Word to prove their case.

More Targets for Deception

Why? Because they are deceived. The spirit of this world has crippled their minds, blinding them to the truth.

Not long ago, we had a funeral for one of our church members, a young mother and wife who was killed by a drunk driver. It was tragic, seeing the lifeless body in that gloomy casket before her "time." Weeping children, crying husband, unfinished work . . . all left behind because of a drunk.

Just one month later, a friend of mine lost two relatives in a disastrous accident involving a drunk driver.

And think of it, that demonic drink which has caused untold heartache, broken homes, sickness, and death is being accepted and even promoted as desirable by foolish, deceived professing believers.

It's no wonder that drinking establishments are losing law suits regularly for serving liquor to drivers. And even wedding parties are being sued for serving beer, wine, and liquor to drivers who murder while "under the influence of alcohol."

Why do you think they call alcoholic drinks "spirits?" It's a dead give away. It's because there's a "demon" in every drink, and if you want to drink him down and let him become a part of your life, you'll suffer immeasurable grief.

> Whose heart is filled with anguish and sorrow? Who is always fighting and quarreling? Who is the man with bloodshot eyes and many wounds? It is the one who spends long hours in the taverns, trying out

Deception, Delusion & Destruction

> new mixtures. Don't let the sparkle and the smooth taste of strong wine deceive you. For in the end it bites like a poisonous serpent; it stings like an adder. You will see hallucinations and have delirium tremens, and you will say foolish, silly things that would embarrass you no end when sober. You will stagger like a sailor tossed at sea, clinging to a swaying mast. And afterwards you will say, "I didn't even know it when they beat me up. ... Let's go and have another drink!"
>
> — Proverbs 23:29-36 (TLB)

DECEPTION! It's true . . . alcohol deceives.

We are in a race. God called us to run the race, and win the race. And you don't win a race by sitting in the grandstands sipping a cocktail, watching others run.

> Know ye not that they which run in a race run all, but one receiveth the prize? So run, that ye may obtain. And every man that striveth for the mastery is temperate in all things. Now they do it to obtain a corruptible crown; but we an incorruptible. I therefore so run, not as uncertainly; so fight I, not as one that beateth the air: But I keep under my body, and bring it into subjection: lest that by any means, when I have preached to others, I myself should be a castaway.
>
> — I Corinthians 9:24-27

Get on the track. Run with the team. Keep going for Jesus, and deception will be left behind in your trail of dust.

Remember ...

More Targets for Deception

☑ 1. Classes of deceived Christians:

   a) Those who hear, but do not obey God's Word.
   b) Christians with licentious attitudes.
   c) Those who disbelieve the law of sowing and reaping.
   d) Those who have an improper concept of riches.
   e) Those who fail in character development.
   f) Those who hate others.
   g) Those living in careless ease.
   h) Drinkers

☑ 2. Some in the last days will unsuspectingly depart from the faith . . . and fall away.

☑ 3. We are in a race. We must win!

Chapter Six:
Who is the Master-Mind Behind Deception?

My family loves animals.

While on a trip to Oklahoma City, we visited the Oklahoma Zoo.

I'm always impressed with the reptiles. Some are beautiful, some colorful, others ugly and sort of colorless. But I noticed a fascinatingly beautiful, almost fluorescent-looking, green snake in one of the glass cages. It was small and harmless looking. But as I read the information about this creature, chills went up my spine.

It was a Green Mamba from East Africa. The card said it was one of the deadliest snakes in the world. In fact, a victim will have less than thirty minutes to live after being bitten by the green reptile.

A missionary friend recently told me about a hunter in a Tanzanian jungle who was bitten on the wrist by one of these small, green snakes. The man, in a panic gesture to save his life, immediately whacked off his own arm with hopes of preventing the poison from

37

Deception, Delusion & Destruction

reaching his heart and brain. Some of the natives say amputation is the only way to prevent death after being struck by a Green Mamba. But the amputation must occur within seconds of the bite or it's too late.

How can something so small and beautiful be so deadly?

That's like deception. Thoughts, attitudes, and practices that seem harmless, even attractive, can actually lead to the deadly bite of deception.

Who . . . or what is behind deception? Is there a spiritual "Green Mamba" trying to lure people into deception and destruction? The answer is yes!

Interestingly, in the third chapter of Genesis we see Satan in the form of a serpent — a snake. In the book of Revelation, he is called a serpent — a snake. What is the nature of the serpent? To deceive and destroy!

> And the great dragon was cast out, THAT OLD SERPENT, called the Devil, and Satan, which DECEIVETH the whole world: he was cast out into the earth, and his angels were cast out with him.
> — Revelation 12:9

> And DECEIVETH them that dwell on the earth by the means of those miracles which he had power to do in the sight of the beast; saying to them that dwell on the earth, that they should make an image to the beast, which had the wound by a sword, and did live.
> — Revelation 13:14

Who is the Master-Mind Behind Deception?

> And cast him into the bottomless pit, and shut him up, and set a seal upon him, that he should DECEIVE the nations no more, till the thousand years should be fulfilled: and after that he must be loosed a little season.
>
> And (Satan) shall go out to DECEIVE the nations which are in the four quarters of the earth, Gog and Magog, to gather them together to battle: the number of whom is as the sand of the sea.
>
> And the devil that DECEIVED them was cast into the lake of fire and brimstone, where the beast and the false prophet are, and shall be tormented day and night forever and ever.
> — Revelation 20:3,8,10 (parenthesis mine)

Deception, however, is not a part of *God's* nature at all. In fact, He abhors it (Psalm 5:6), Jesus was completely free of it (I Peter 2:22), and a curse is pronounced on ministers who try to do God's work using deception (Jeremiah 48:10).

Satan, the devil, is behind all forms of deception. He lures people off target now, just a little, so they'll be miles off in the months and years ahead, and eventually be thrust into a blistering hell packed with demonic creatures. Satan searches for a way to somehow snag a hook in the life of the believer for the purpose of destroying him. (I Peter 5:8)

The devil hates Jesus Christ and all of mankind. He is out to steal, kill, and destroy (John 10:10). But he must first get a hook in your jaw, to lure you toward his deadly bite of deception.

Why is deception so dreadfully serious? Because . . .

Deception, Delusion & Destruction

... First, you don't realize you're being deceived.

... Secondly, it brings serious complications into your life.

... Thirdly, it blinds, binds, and destroys you.

... Finally, the day will come when it's too late to turn back.

> Even him, whose coming is after the working of Satan with all power and signs and lying wonders, and with all deceivableness of unrighteousness in them that perish; because they received not the love of the truth, that they might be saved. And for this cause God shall send them strong delusion, that they should believe a lie.
> — II Thessalonians 2:9-11

The end result of deception is damnation; to be eternally separated from God, to suffer the torments and horrors of an eternal hell. Jesus spoke more about hell than he did about heaven. He did this, perhaps, to emphasize the necessity of shunning deceptive attitudes and practices that could lead your soul to the place of torture prepared for the devil and his angels. (Matthew 25:41)

Satan desires to humiliate you and publicly disgrace you. Listen to the words of a young man who was deceived, then bitten by the deadly serpent:

> "Oh, if only I had listened! If only I had not demanded my own way! Oh, why wouldn't I take advice? Why was I so stupid?"
> — Proverbs 5:12-13 (TLB)

Who is the Master-Mind Behind Deception?

Satan lures with the lie, "Just one time, that's all." Then, he says, "Just one more time. You can stop anytime you want." Soon a cable of sin and deception is woven around your mind and life. You are snared — trapped! Bitten by the deadly serpent of deception.

> "Come on, let's take our fill of love until morning."
> — Proverbs 7:18 (TLB)

"Just until morning. Then you can stop." But soon you discover that you can't stop. The poison of deception is already beginning to paralyze you. Another victim! You!

Satan is suggestive. He made a suggestion to Judas Iscariot. He suggested that Judas could make a little extra money by betraying Jesus.

> During supper the devil had already suggested to Judas Iscariot, Simon's son, that this was the night to carry out his plan to betray Jesus.
> — John 13:2 (TLB)

The plan seemed innocent. I'm sure Judas didn't realize the magnitude of his deception, and the resulting consequences.

> And Judas Iscariot, one of the twelve, went unto the chief priests, to betray Him unto them. And when they heard it, they were glad and promised to give him money. And he sought how he might conveniently betray Him.
> — Mark 14:10-11

But look at the words Jesus spoke concerning the one who walked into this tragic trap of deception:

Deception, Delusion & Destruction

> The Son of man indeed goeth, as it is written of him: but woe to that man by whom the Son of man is betrayed! Good were it for that man if he had never been born.
>
> — Mark 14:21

It would have been better if Judas had never been born! Why? Because right now he sits, tormented, among the damned of the ages, awaiting his awful judgment when he'll be assigned to a flaming hell for all eternity.

Once a successful minister, Judas now waits incarcerated with Adolf Hitler, Benito Mussolini, Pontius Pilate, Joseph Stalin, and the other vile and wicked beings who died without Christ.

I've studied the stages of Judas' betrayal. It started as a small deception.

1. *Dissatisfaction.* Things weren't being operated the way he thought they should be.

2. *Fault-finding.* Judas began complaining.

3. *He justified his "little" sins.* He was stealing from the treasury and justifying himself.

4. *He warmed up to the enemies of Christ.* (Mark 14:10)

5. *He started searching for the right time and right place to commit his act of treason.* (Some search for the right time and place to sin.)

Who is the Master-Mind Behind Deception?

6. *He believed a reward would await him if he acted.*

7. *He developed utter hypocrisy.* (He kissed Jesus, his one-time friend and leader, while betraying Him.)

DECEIVED! LOST! FOREVER!

The great deceiver, the devil, MUST BE RESISTED! Peter gives us a simple, but powerful action plan:

> Be sober, be vigilant; because your adversary the devil, as a roaring lion, walketh about, seeking whom he may devour: Whom resist stedfast in the faith, knowing that the same afflictions are accomplished in your brethren that are in the world.
> — I Peter 5:8-9

1. *Be sober.*

2. *Be vigilant.* Why? Because the master-deceiver is stalking you, desiring to destroy you through deception.

3. *Resist!*

4. *Remain steadfast in the faith.*

5. *Know that you're not the only one.* Others are facing deceptive opportunities also.

In Proverbs 5:7-14 (TLB) we are told the results of being deceived into some sin:

1. You'll lose your honor.

Deception, Delusion & Destruction

2. You'll give the remainder of your life to the cruel and merciless.

3. Someone else will get your wealth.

4. You'll become a slave.

5. You'll groan in anguish and shame.

6. You'll say, "I wish I'd listened."

7. You'll face public disgrace.

Who is the deceiver? Satan himself, God's archenemy. He seeks to shame, disgrace, and humiliate the believer. Thus, his plan of deception. It works well on those believers who aren't seriously practicing the principles taught in I Peter 5:8-9.

In our Bible Training Institute, I teach a class on practical pastoral ministries. In the class we study the lives of successful men of God, who overcame all sorts of obstacles and temptations, and went on to shake cities and nations for Christ. We also study those who have fallen through moral or financial failure. There is a pattern for success and a pattern for failure.

The pattern for failure is always the same. Deception creeps in somewhere. One greatly used man of God began overworking. His prayer life dwindled. Because of his great success, he began to believe the suggestion that he was the prophesied Elijah who would appear prior to the coming of Christ. He died deceived, broken, and penniless. SHAMED. DISGRACED!

Who is the Master-Mind Behind Deception?

Another one-time "super star" for God failed to allow the Holy Spirit to continue His sanctifying work. He believed the lie that a little drink now and then is okay, "... Just to calm the nerves." He was arrested for drunk driving. Later he died in shame with sclerosis of the liver, caused by his continued drunkenness. DECEPTION ALWAYS HURTS.

Just the other day, I sat at breakfast with a man who was an associate minister at one of the great churches in our nation. The pastor was caught in an adulterous affair, lost his pastorate, shamed his family, and is on the proverbial scrap heap today. I asked what had happened. It was discovered that the man continued to read pornographic material with little or no restraint. He was deceived into believing that his little sin would not manifest itself in larger sins. DECEIVED! DESTROYED! BROKEN! DISGRACED!

Others have been deceived by riches or power. The end is the same. SHAME and DISGRACE.

VIPER EGGS

> They trust in empty words and speak lies; they conceive evil and bring forth iniquity. They hatch viper's eggs and weave the spider's web; he who eats of their eggs dies, and from that which is crushed a viper breaks out.
> — Isaiah 59:4b-5 (NKJV)

When believers are deceived into allowing "little sins" to remain unchecked and unrepented of, they will eventually hatch vipers — snakes! Deadly spiritual Green Mambas!

Deception, Delusion & Destruction

Dear friend, if you are walking in some form of deception right now, I pray the Holy Spirit will agitate your spirit so you know it and deal with it. The devil — the spiritual Green Mamba — will say, "Take care of it tomorrow." But God's Word says "TODAY is the day of salvation (or deliverance)."

TODAY, ask God to forgive you. Make no excuses. Come clean with God and take His antidote to the poison of deception and sin. The antidote: FAITH IN THE CLEANSING AND KEEPING POWER OF THE BLOOD OF JESUS CHRIST! Confess your sin and deception now — and be free, in Jesus' name.

> (For he saith, I have heard thee in a time accepted, and in the day of salvation have I succoured thee: behold, now is the accepted time; behold, NOW is the day of salvation.)
> — II Corinthians 6:2

> While it is said, TODAY if ye will hear his voice, harden not your hearts, as in the provocation.
> — Hebrews 3:15

> Seeing then that we have a great high priest, that is passed into the heavens, Jesus the Son of God, let us hold fast our profession. For we have not an high priest which cannot be touched with the feeling of our infirmities; but was in all points tempted like as we are, yet without sin. Let us therefore come boldly unto the throne of grace, that we may obtain mercy, and find grace to help in time of need.
> — Hebrews 4:14-16

> For I will be merciful to their unrighteousness, and their sins and their iniquities will I remember no more.
> — Hebrews 8:12

Who is the Master-Mind Behind Deception?

> How much more shall the blood of Christ, who through the eternal Spirit offered himself without spot to God, purge your conscience from dead works to serve the living God?
> — Hebrews 9:14

The deceiver wants to cheat you of joy, peace, success, and real freedom. He wants to ensnare and bind you, causing you to wander aimlessly, never genuinely satisfied.

Church people who wander from church to church all their lives are likely walking in deception. They've allowed themselves to be bitten by a spiritual Green Mamba. But they don't believe it. DECEIVED!

In the next chapter we'll discuss the most dangerous form of deception — religious deception.

Remember...

☑ 1. Small deceptions can be deadly.

☑ 2. There is a spiritual "Green Mamba." His name is Satan.

☑ 3. Satan is the master-mind behind all forms of deception.

☑ 4. Satan wants to humiliate and publicly disgrace you. That's why he has a program of deception.

☑ 5. The seven stages to Judas' betrayal:

   a) Dissatisfaction. Things weren't being operated the way he thought they should be.

Deception, Delusion & Destruction

- b) Fault-finding. Judas began complaining.
- c) He justified his "little" sins. He was stealing from the treasury and justifying himself.
- d) He warmed up to the enemies of Christ (Mark 14:10).
- e) He started searching for the right time and right place to commit his act of treason. (Some search for the right time and place to sin.)
- f) He believed a reward would await him if he acted.
- g) He developed utter hypocrisy. (He kissed Jesus, his one-time friend and leader, while betraying Him.)

☑ 6. The seven-fold cost of permitting deception:

- a) You'll lose your honor.
- b) You'll give the remainder of your life to the cruel and merciless.
- c) Someone else will get your wealth.
- d) You'll become a slave.
- e) You'll groan in anguish and shame.
- f) You'll say, "I wish I'd listened."
- g) You'll face pubic disgrace.

☑ 7. Patterns for failure are all the same. Deception!

☑ 8. *Today,* God will deliver you from deception if you will go to Him, trusting in the Blood of His Son, Jesus Christ.

Chapter Seven: Religious Deception

People are looking for answers to their problems. And today scores of television advertisements offer "solutions" to those problems. For example, I recently saw an advertisement offering New Age healing crystals, claiming to promote mysterious cures for sickness and disease.

Another contemporary advertisement is aimed at the hurting family. It's an advertisement produced by a quality agency, very emotional and heart warming. But it promotes a growing world-wide cult which worships a different Jesus than the Bible Jesus. They believe Lucifer is Jesus' brother, and that "born again" means you'll be born again on another planet after you die. Their ad campaign is a part of an end-time strategy to boost membership in their cult, and of course, countless thousands are being drawn in by the deception because they offer solutions through their religious system.

Deception, Delusion & Destruction

> Now the Spirit speaketh expressly, that in the latter times some shall depart from the faith, giving heed to seducing spirits, and doctrines of devils; Speaking lies in hypocrisy; having their conscience seared with a hot iron.
>
> — I Timothy 4:1-2

There is a type of deception that seems to be deeper and stronger than any other deception known. It's called religious deception.

Millions of people gather weekly to worship a God they don't know. Millions practice rituals and ceremonies, hoping to appease a god who is never satisfied. This deception — religious deception — is so deep and so terrible, it is like no other deception. Religious deception hardens one's heart to true faith. The traditions practiced in various religions make God's Word of no effect.

> Making the Word of God of none effect through your tradition . . . .
>
> — Mark 7:13a

Religious deception builds serious psychological complexes into the minds of those it holds captive.

Why is there so much deception? I saw pop singer, Tina Turner on a talk show recently. Tina made a tremendous comeback after her separation from Ike. She elaborated on her dreadful, heart-breaking story of how her husband severely beat her, time after time, and how she plummeted to the depths of despair. When the host asked her who she credits for her successful comeback, she responded, "Buddhism." She gave the credit to her studies in Buddhism.

John Denver, the pop star who made the popular

Religious Deception

hit "Almost Heaven, West Virginia," tells us that transcendental meditation (a soft-colored form of Hinduism) is the secret of success.

DECEPTION! RELIGIOUS DECEPTION!

Some may accuse me of teaching a negative message here. "Very close-minded." My friend, I'm giving you a positive message of hope and reality. This message will keep you from seducing spirits and doctrines of demons, and keep you on the narrow road to success, joy, peace, and eternal life. Those other roads lead to destruction.

> Enter ye in at the strait gate: for wide is the gate, and broad is the way, that leadeth to destruction, and many there be which go in thereat: Because strait is the gate, and narrow is the way, which leadeth unto life, and few there be that find it.
>
> — Matthew 7:13-14

Some people think that dabbling in false religions really doesn't matter. A prominent preacher on the Phil Donahue program said, "There are many roads that lead to God, and Jesus is one of those roads." That preacher is a false prophet, deceiving thousands, while he professes to be a Christian minister.

You see, Jesus Himself told us in plain language that He is the only way to experience real life now, and eternal life with Him later. There's only one road to God, and that's Jesus!

> Jesus saith unto him, I am the way, the truth, and the life: no man cometh unto the Father, but by me.
>
> — John 14:6

Deception, Delusion & Destruction

> For there is one God, and one mediator between God and men, the man Christ Jesus.
> — I Timothy 2:5

Satan is behind every diversion from the truth. He is behind every false religious system, every false belief, and every false cult today. His plan is to entangle people in religion to keep them from the simple truth that faith in Christ leads to real freedom.

> But I fear, lest by any means, as the serpent beguiled Eve through his subtlety, so your minds should be corrupted from the simplicity that is in Christ.
> — II Corinthians 11:3

I saw an interview with a woman who had pursued false religions until she became so deceived and disillusioned, that she ended up in a satanic worship cult. She told a mind-boggling story of a ritual in which a human sacrifice, her own infant son, was made to Satan. She considered it a high honor.

The satanists stripped until they were completely nude. Then they set little Michael in the middle of the room with other children, four to six years old, placed in an inner circle around Michael. All the children were given knives and were told to throw them at little Michael. They were commanded with threats from the adults to perform this horrible act of violence.

The children began throwing the knives at Michael. The little fellow was screaming, but his cries were drowned out by the satanic chanting of the worshippers. More knives were given, then thrown. Blood was all over the place. Finally Michael died.

Religious Deception

Theodore, Michael's brother, who was forced to participate in this bloody ritual, somehow got to the authorities and reported what had happened. He said, "My little baby brother is dead, but mommy says it's Jesus who is dead. She and her friends keep saying 'Baby Jesus is dead. Baby Jesus is dead.'"

This is a true account of blatant satanism. Serious? You bet! But that same Satan who possessed these people to murder, is the same creature behind every false religion, practice, system, and belief, from astrology to humanism to satanism.

I'm telling you the devil is nobody to play around with. Whether it's astrology, spiritism, consulting a fortune teller, having your palms read, having someone read your tarot cards... it is all the same force: the deceiving work of the devil. When you play with the devil and give him a place in your life, you begin to open yourself up to all kinds of masterful deceptions. Small religious deceptions will one day grow into full-blown cases of delusion.

Satan is a mastermind. And if you think religious deception is confusing today, just wait until the days ahead. There's going to be religious deception everywhere. Every one of us in Christ's Church has to develop discerning hearts. WE HAVE TO BE ABLE TO RECOGNIZE WOLVES IN SHEEP'S CLOTHING so that we're not caught up and led astray by these false ministers.

> For many shall come in my name, saying, I am Christ; and shall deceive many.
> — Matthew 24:5

How many shall come in His name? *Many* shall come in Christ's name and shall deceive many. In Matthew 7:15, Jesus said:

> Beware [in Greek: shun, avoid, stay away from, run from, have nothing to do with] of false prophets, which come to you in sheep's clothing, but inwardly they are ravening wolves. Ye shall know them by their fruits. Do men gather grapes of thorns, or figs of thistles? Even so every good tree bringeth forth good fruit; but a corrupt tree bringeth forth evil fruit. A good tree cannot bring forth evil fruit, neither can a corrupt tree bring forth good fruit. Every tree that bringeth not forth good fruit is hewn down, and cast into the fire. Wherefore by their fruits ye shall know them.
> — Matthew 7:15-20

Notice, you SHALL NOT know them by their miracles. You SHALL NOT know them by the great things they are able to do. You SHALL NOT know them by their charisma. You SHALL know them by their FRUITS. Verse 21:

> Not everyone that saith unto me, Lord, Lord, shall enter into the kingdom of heaven; but he that doeth the will of my Father which is in heaven. Many will say to me in that day, Lord, Lord, have we not prophesied in thy name? and in thy name have cast out devils? and in thy name done many wonderful works?
> — Matthew 7:21-22

Jesus said MANY will come in His name and deceive many. They'll say, "I come in Jesus' name and prophesy, and cast out devils, and in His name, do many wonderful works."

Religious Deception

And then will I profess unto them, I never knew you; depart form me, ye that work iniquity.
— Matthew 7:23

In Acts 20, Paul gives a message to every caring pastor of every church. He says:

Take heed therefore unto yourselves, and to all the flock, over which the Holy Ghost hath made you overseers, to feed the church of God, which He hath purchased with His own blood. For I know this, that after my departing shall grievous wolves enter in among you, not sparing the flock. Also of your own selves shall men arise, speaking perverse [perverted] things, to draw away disciples after them. Therefore watch, and remember, that by the space of three years I ceased not to warn every one night and day with tears.
— Acts 20:28-31

For such are false apostles, deceitful workers, transforming themselves into the apostles of Christ. And no marvel; for Satan himself is transformed into an angel of light. Therefore it is no great thing if his ministers also be transformed as the ministers of righteousness; whose end shall be according to their works.
— II Corinthians 11:13

Now the Spirit speaketh expressly that in the latter times some shall depart from the faith, giving heed to seducing spirits, and doctrines of devils; Speaking lies in hypocrisy; having their conscience seared with a hot iron.
— I Timothy 4:1

But there were false prophets also among the people, even as there shall be false teachers among you, who privily shall bring in damnable heresies,

Deception, Delusion & Destruction

even denying the Lord that bought them, and bring upon themselves swift destruction. And many shall follow their pernicious ways; by reason of whom the way of truth shall be evil spoken of.
— II Peter 2:1

Do you know that because of false teachers and false prophets true Christianity is evil spoken of? The Bible lists false christs, false apostles, false prophets, false teachers, false brethren. Everywhere it says BEWARE. What is a false minister? He's one who claims to have a message, a revelation, or a teaching from God, but really doesn't. Jesus said to YOU, beware. We are each individually responsible to avoid deception.

Forty thousand cults are flourishing in the United States of America today. Eighty percent of the membership of those cults are made up of people who were once adherents of orthodox Christianity. That's what the Bible calls "departing from the faith." They've departed from the doctrine of Christ and followed after a demon-inspired doctrine.

Watch out for the false leaders — and there are many of them around — who don't believe that Jesus Christ came to earth as a human being with a body like ours. Such people are against the truth and against Christ. Beware of being like them, and losing the prize that you and I have been working so hard to get. See to it that you win our full reward from the Lord. For if you wander beyond the teaching of Christ, you will leave God behind; while if you are loyal to Christ's teaching, you will have God too. Then you will have both the Father and the Son. If anyone comes to teach you, and he doesn't believe what Christ taught, don't even invite him into your home. Don't encourage him in any way. If you do you will be a partner with him in his wickedness.
— II John 7-11 (TLB)

THINGS TO LOOK FOR IN A CHURCH

You may wonder how to protect yourself from religious deception. Here's a check list of important things to look for in a church:

☑ 1. Salvation is by faith in the shed Blood of Jesus Christ. It is a work of grace, not human effort.

☑ 2. The Bible is the Inspired Word of God, from Genesis to Revelation.

☑ 3. God is eternally existent in three Persons: God the Father, God the Son, and God the Holy Spirit. This is known as the Trinity; the Triune God.

☑ 4. The Holy Spirit baptism.

☑ 5. Divine healing.

☑ 6. Mission-mindedness. (Make sure your church believes in and supports missionary projects.)

☑ 7. Evangelism. (Make sure your church believes in and *practices* soul winning.)

☑ 8. The *imminent* return of the Lord Jesus Christ.

Beware of so-called ministers who deny any of the cardinal doctrines of the Christian faith. They are not ministers of God, but of Satan!

Deception, Delusion & Destruction

BEWARE OF "MINISTERS" WHO DENY:

☑ 1. The Virgin birth of Christ.

☑ 2. The Deity of Christ. (Deity means that Jesus Christ is actually God. Jesus was NOT a man who became God through "initiations." He was not an archangel. He is God, the Second Person of the Trinity.)

☑ 3. The Blood Atonement.

☑ 4. The death, burial, and resurrection of Christ.

☑ 5. Christ's miracle-working power today.

☑ 6. The imminent return of Jesus Christ.

☑ 7. The inspired Word of God.

☑ 8. Everlasting life for the saved and everlasting punishment of the unsaved.

And, what about the character, the life-style of a true minister? Please understand, not one of us is perfect yet. We all still have struggles from time-to-time, including authentic servants of Christ. But our life-style should be one of holiness. Does the preacher turn people from sin? Or does he tolerate practices condemned by God's Word?

Men standing in our pulpits ought to have character above good preaching abilities. It makes no difference if he can sway a crowd or raise money, if he doesn't have character (good fruit) the Bible says he's a false leader. I have studied about false prophets and false

Religious Deception

teachers, and discovered that the Bible says very little about their teaching or preaching abilities. It mostly points to their shabby character. You don't always recognize false leaders by their teaching, you recognize them by their character. Do they love their wives? Are they walking in holiness and purity? God looks at the character.

I heard a story about a man whose son was a builder. "Son," he said, "I want you to build a house. I'm giving you $400,000 and I want you to build the finest house this money can build. We're building it for a very special client."

So the young builder took the money from his dad and began working on the house. But, instead of constructing "fine quality" as his father had requested, the son cut corners. He used cheap materials, and "drank up" whatever excess money he could scalp from the special client's house.

Finally the job was complete, although substandard. "The house is finished," the builder told his dad. When the father heard the news, he replied, "Son I've had you build this house for YOURSELF. It is my gift to YOU."

Character has a way of catching up to us.

THE BIBLE HAS MORE TO SAY ABOUT FALSE RELIGIOUS LEADERS

☑ 1. *They may come in sheep's clothing.*

That is, you can't recognize false ministers just by looking at them. They may dress nicely. They may look nice. They may slap on some after-shave lotion and

Deception, Delusion & Destruction

smell nice. They may talk nice. They may even say, "Praise the Lord." They may know all the Christian jargon. They may look like sheep. But Jesus said you won't be able to recognize false religious leaders just by looking at them. They come in sheep's clothing in order to deceive, but inwardly they are ravening wolves.

☑ 2. *They may have charisma and power but not the character of Christ.*

They can imitate miracles. They can imitate gifts of the Spirit, but they cannot imitate the fruit of the Spirit. Moses was the meekest man on earth and he performed miracles. The false prophets of Pharaoh's kingdom were the most arrogant people on the earth and they worked miracles too. You see, Moses had the miracles with the character; the false prophets had miracles but no character. So you can't judge merely by outward appearance. You can't judge just by a miracle or some supernatural-looking gift.

☑ 3. *They may speak perverse things.*

They will likely distort the truth in order to draw away disciples after themselves.

☑ 4. *They may claim apostolic authority, therefore are accountable to no man.*

A man walked up to me after church one Sunday and asked, "If I join this church, will I have to come under your authority?"

I responded, "Well, of course. I'm the pastor of this church, the overseer of this flock, and if you become a member of this church, you're going to be one of the

Religious Deception

sheep and will come under the authority of the pastor."

He stared at me with a perplexed look and blurted out, "That cannot be possible because Jesus Christ Himself has sent me into the world as an apostle with much more authority than you. So how can I submit to you?"

I looked at him and said, "You don't have anything from Jesus Christ. You're deceived by the devil." He shrugged his shoulders and walked away.

☑ 5. *They may claim to be ministers of righteousness.*

They may even wear religious symbols in order to deceive.

☑ 6. *They are led by seducing spirits and teach doctrines of demons.*

☑ 7. *They speak lies with straight faces.*

A GOOD GUARD AGAINST RELIGIOUS DECEPTION

The best way to guard yourself from false religions, cults, and false teachers is to study the genuine. Go to God's Word and see what a genuine church looks like. Study true ministers such as St. Paul and St. Peter. Were they perfect? No, but they spoke the truth and were developing in character.

When you study the genuine, then you'll be able to recognize the counterfeits.

Deception, Delusion & Destruction

That's what the U.S. Treasury Department does. They make their people study genuine U.S. bills so that when a counterfeit comes along, no matter what kind of counterfeit it is, they will instantly be able to recognize it. They know the genuine.

How do you recognize religious deceivers? In the next chapter I'll give some danger signs. Study them carefully, because I guarantee, you'll need to know them as we approach the final hours before Christ's coming.

Remember ...

☑ 1. Religious deception is stronger and deeper than any other kind.

☑ 2. Satan is behind every diversion from the truth.

☑ 3. Small religious deceptions grow into full-blown cases of delusion.

☑ 4. False ministers may carry the label "Christian."

☑ 5. Jesus said we are individually responsible to avoid deception. He said YOU are to beware.

Chapter Eight: Danger Signs

How do you recognize religious deceivers? I'm going to give you some danger signs right now. Jot these signs down on a piece of paper because I promise you, you're going to need them in the future. Keep them with your Bible or put them in your wallet. They're going to help you.

One of the first ways that you can recognize religious deceivers is:

☑ 1. *There is an exclusiveness about them.*

In other words, they seem to divide the body of Christ. They may promote their group as an exclusive remnant of the Church. They have difficulty recognizing other legitimate expressions of Christ's body. If they do happen to view other Christians as semi-genuine, they'll subtly undermine them.

For example, they will say things like this: "Oh, yes, that's a church all right. But it's too bad they don't have the deep revelation that we have." There's almost

Deception, Delusion & Destruction

an arrogance about them.

Deceivers foster the attitude that they are leading the only true remnant of believers. Others are apostate. In fact, oftentimes they'll speak evil of God's anointed servants, hoping to elevate themselves while isolating their followers from mainstream Christianity:

> Likewise also these filthy dreamers defile the flesh, despise dominion, and speak evil of dignities.
> —Jude 8

Jude tells us these deceivers reject authority and speak evil of dignitaries, or God's anointed ones.

Why do they do it? Because they can't draw a crowd after themselves by telling people to support other evangelists and to read other Christian books. So they start undermining authentic ministries by finding fault with them.

I read a magazine by an evangelist who was living in immorality. It wasn't known at the time, but later he admitted it. Anyway, I saw two major danger signs in his writings. First, he claimed to be the only one left who could evangelize the world. Secondly, he blasted other ministries *by name*, trying to make them look like New Age adherents because of the terminology they used in their sermons.

In one article he lambasted the concept of envisioning answers to your prayers. He said it was an occultic practice. In the very same issue of his magazine, he was giving a testimony of how he had prayed and saw the answer with his "eye of faith." Tell me,

Danger Signs

what's the difference if one evangelist says, "I envisioned the answer," and another evangelist says, "I saw the answer with my 'eye of faith'?" It sounds pretty much like the same thing to me, yet this immoral evangelist used it as an opportunity to find fault with other ministries, most likely in hopes of developing an "exclusiveness" — remnant mind-set in his followers.

Oftentimes, deceivers will take Old Testament Scriptures out of context and "spiritualize" them to mean something other than God had intended. When they do this, they convince their followers that the whole Church is in a backslidden condition, except for the "faithful remnant." Of course, the "faithful remnant" is made up of their loyal followers only.

> These are spots in your feasts of charity, when they feast with you, feeding themselves without fear: clouds they are without water, carried about of winds; trees whose fruit withereth, without fruit, TWICE DEAD, plucked up by the roots; Raging waves of the sea, foaming out their own shame; wandering stars, to whom is reserved the blackness of darkness for ever.
>
> —Jude 12-13

I've seen it happen time and time again, and one of the most alarming facts that I have found about this exclusiveness is that these deceivers often come from within good churches. They were, at one time, good ministers; good men of God. But Jude calls them "twice dead." That means they were born again. They had died to their life of sin, but for some reason they went back into their life of sin and died again. Twice dead!

Paul says they come from among us and speak perverse things such as: "We are the 144,000. Oh, yes,

Deception, Delusion & Destruction

we believe God blesses other churches, but our church is the chosen 144,000 of Revelation. Only the 144,000 are going to make it into heaven. Everyone else will be annihilated."

That practice is known as spiritualizing Scriptures! Why don't people just take the Word of God for what it says? Why do they have to say, "An angel came into my bedroom and explained this Scripture to me. The 144,000 will be those who follow my ministry."?

Quite frankly I wouldn't even want to be one of the 144,000. They'll be here during the Great Tribulation, but I suppose some false teachers have spiritualized the Tribulation away. I have listened to teachers in utter amazement as they say we are now in the Millennial Age. Well, if we're in the Millennium and the devil is bound, why is there so much sickness? Why is there so much sin? Why are there still murders? Why are there still such hideous practices going on in this earth if the devil is already bound?

The Bible tells us that in the Millennial Age, the lion is going to lay down with the lamb. I can't even get my cat to lay down with the neighbor's dog. False prophets. False teachers. Developing that exclusiveness.

A few years ago some of these "exclusive" believers started visiting our church, probably to proselytize. I called one of them into my office to confront him about his false concept of the so-called "seven steps to perfection." I explained to him that these were deceptive and false teachings. He arrogantly responded, "I'm sorry, man. You just don't have the light on it. You just don't have the revelation that our group is the 'man child'

Danger Signs

and your church is the 'son-clad woman'." (All this spiritualizing from the book of Revelation.) I said to him, "Brother, listen. I love you. I want you to come to this church, but that group you are getting into has an air of exclusiveness; a 'we four — and no more,' attitude. It's not God."

Now that's hard to do as a pastor. But when I see sheep getting close to the cliff and ready to fall over among ravening wolves, I try to jerk them back into the flock. Sometimes it seems awful unkind of me to pull them by their necks and say, "Get back in here." But I love them and I have no greater joy than when the sheep are walking in the truth. But, if I've done my best and they still choose to jump over there among the wolves, there is nothing more I can do about it.

I told one fellow that I had God's Word, the Bible, as my revelation. He responded, "Oh, but my revelation goes deeper than that." Deeper than the Bible? If your revelation goes deeper than God's Word, you've got the wrong revelation!

He says, "No, no. What I mean is you've got to get the revelation on the revelation of revelation." Now I want you to know that I believe in revelation. I believe in revelation knowledge from the Holy Spirit, but it had better not contradict what's already written in God's Word. It had better line up. If it doesn't; if it spiritualizes the Scriptures and make them say something they don't say, it's not revelation from God. It's from a fallen angel of light seeking to deceive.

Believe me, lives can be devastated by deception. Joy vanishes. Deceived people don't even know why their joy is gone, but I'll tell you why it's gone: The devil

Deception, Delusion & Destruction

came to steal, kill and destroy. He's out to destroy your joy. He's out to kill your happiness. He's out to ruin your holiness. He's out to make you miserable because he hates God. We say the devil hates you. He really doesn't hate you. The fact is, he doesn't care anything at all about you. He has no feelings for you whatsoever. At least hatred is a feeling. He has no emotions for you. He hates God and knows it will hurt God if he can hurt you. Religious deception will run rampant in the final hours of history. Watch out for that exclusiveness. Don't divide the body of Christ.

A journalist for the local paper came over and interviewed me some time ago. She also interviewed two other pastors in our township. Those other pastors, in the report, said nice things about me and Mount Hope Church. And when the reporter was here, I said nice things about those other churches. Do you know why? Because I know that Jesus Christ is Lord at those other two churches. I know the pastors are winning souls to Jesus Christ and I recognize them as legitimate parts of the body of Christ, even though we are of different denominations. I love them, and they love me.

Don't divide the body of Christ. Watch out for those with an air of exclusiveness who try to divide the body of Christ. The body is not divided.

☑ 2. *They generally major on minor issues rather than on the person and work of Jesus Christ.*

There are some churches where, 52 weeks out of the year, the preacher will get up and speak against some other church, or some minor issues of no real consequence. When you're called of God to tell people

Danger Signs

about Jesus Christ, and to preach the Gospel, don't use your pulpit as a soap box to run everybody down.

I flew down to Kentucky for just a few hours to conduct a funeral in Louisville. A lady approached me after the funeral and said, "That was really good. It spoke to my heart. I go to church in Louisville. I'm a Christian." Then all of a sudden she whipped around, looked me in the eye, and blurted out, "In what manner do you baptize?" I said, "We do it in water." Then she said, "But what name do you use?" I said, "We've got all the bases covered when we baptize, dear, because some believe in baptizing in the name of the Father and of the Son and of the Holy Spirit. Others say, 'No, you must baptize in the name of Jesus Christ.' So what we do is baptize in the name of God the Father, Jesus Christ the Son, and God the Holy Spirit. We got it all covered in one." She didn't know what to say then.

I'm amazed at how many people will make a major issue out of something minor. Baptism is an act of obedience. It demonstrates a willingness to follow Jesus Christ by acting on His command to be baptized. The important thing is not the exact words that are used. The important thing is going down under that water. If a church dunks people three times in the name of the Father and of the Son and of the Holy Spirit, or once in the name of God the Father, Jesus Christ the Son, and God the Holy Spirit, what difference does it make? Just dunk them!

False teachers will major on minor issues. Their focus has shifted from the person and work of Jesus Christ. We're here to honor Jesus Christ, to learn about Him, and to grow in our love for Him.

Deception, Delusion & Destruction

Deceivers focus on minor issues; issues that are not pertinent to salvation, the person, or the work of Jesus Christ.

☑ 3. *There seems to be an emphasis on extra scriptural revelation, or a leader that has some divine inspiration which he claims is equal to the Scriptures.*

False teachers often claim that their words are just as anointed as God's Written Word. Some proclaim that just as the apostle John's words were inspired, so has God inspired their words. They maintain that their words are equal to the words on the pages of the Bible.

I once heard that notion from a Protestant minister who dressed like a priest. He said he was caught up to heaven and . . . "My experience was just as valid as the apostle John's." The only difference is that this minister came back with a truck load of false revelations. His visions were totally contrary to God's Word, but he claimed, "My experience was just as valid as the Apostle John's." So people marvelled, "Oh, this man's been to heaven."

I believe there are men of God who have seen Jesus. There are men of God who have had personal contacts with the Lord in visions. I believe that's true. But when people "come back" speaking false revelations and lies, do you know what they had? They had an experience with an angel of light. Watch out for those who say their words are equal to the Scriptures. They usually have a "new truth," or a "deeper truth." They have light or insight that nobody else has, and they have such a know-it-all, unteachable attitude that you can't help them.

Our Divine Defense Against Deception

For such are false apostles, deceitful workers, transforming themselves into the apostles of Christ. And no marvel; for Satan himself is transformed into an angel of light. Therefore it is no great thing if his ministers also be transformed as the ministers of righteousness; whose end shall be according to their works.

— II Corinthians 11:13-15

There was an extra Scriptural doctrine a few years ago that said when a demon is cast out of you, you will always vomit. At camp meetings, people were given paper bags to vomit in. And this preacher said, "I learned this when I was casting out a demon, he was talking to me, telling me how it was to be done."

Well, to me, that's a teaching of a demon, isn't it? That's a doctrine of a demon. Many shall depart from the faith giving heed to seducing spirits and teachings of demons; doctrines of demons.

"Hey buddy, this is how you cast me out. You get a paper bag, see." Can you feature it? And so they got around in a group and then the teacher announced, "Now some of you have had hatred and bitterness and jealousy. These are all demons that are living in you and they're going to come out when I count to three. You're all going to vomit in your little bags and that will be the demon."

Anybody who didn't vomit was not considered to be delivered. It's funny, but it was an extra scriptural revelation.

Now again, let me balance that out by saying that often times when demons come out of people they will

Deception, Delusion & Destruction

vomit or gag. I was in our auditorium one night and a man was sitting alone in one of the pews. I was all alone. My wife was in the nursery getting our kids. Everybody had gone home. I walked over to the man and said, "You need to accept Jesus Christ." He said, "I can't." I put my hand on his head and said, "In the name of Jesus Christ, devil I bind you. Loose this man now!" He started gagging and choking and letting out blood curdling screams. I believe things like this can happen when people are being delivered. But to make a doctrine out of an experience is extra scriptural revelation. (By the way, the fellow was set free and accepted Christ that night.)

Now I've heard a new one: Dancing with your "spiritual connection." And again, I believe in dancing before the Lord. It's Scriptural. And you don't have to wait for some cloud to come on you that says, "Dance!"

But some preacher has this "new revelation." He says an angel told him, I guess, that you can dance only with your "spiritual connection" (whatever that is). So, they dance around the church with their "spiritual connections." False teachers. Deception will come in the form of extra scriptural revelation.

✓ 4. *There will be some strange twist about the teaching of Jesus Christ or the nature of God.*

One cult today says that Lucifer was Jesus Christ's brother. That puts Jesus Christ on the same level as a created being. Some will twist His deity. Or they will have a bad teaching about his uniqueness. Some say He was 50 percent God and 50 percent man.

Danger Signs

That's what Archie Bunker said on television when he was criticizing the Jews. When "Meathead" replied, "But Jesus was a Jew," Archie quickly voided "Meathead's" argument with the reply, "He was only half Jew."

Well that's not true. Jesus was 100 percent Jew, but he was also 100 percent God. That's the uniqueness of Jesus Christ. He was the only one who has ever been 100 percent God and 100 percent man.

Now today, you and I are 100 percent man and we have 100 percent God living in us. But Jesus was unique. He was 100 percent God and 100 percent man. Mathematically impossible? Yes, with man it's impossible but with God all things are possible.

Deceivers may have a strange twist about Jesus' virgin birth, His death, or His bodily resurrection. There are entire groups that say Jesus never rose from the dead, bodily. "He just rose spiritually from the dead," they claim because, "Jesus made no footprints after he rose from the dead." Where do they get that? False teachers. False teaching. Deception. They're twisting the doctrine of Christ.

Deceivers will misinterpret Christ's physical return to the earth. They talk about the Christ consciousness, the aquarian gospel, but what they're really talking about is a different Jesus. They're not talking about the Jesus of the Bible. It's a different Jesus. There are many Jesuses, but only one Jesus, the Son of the Living God. And that's the One to whom we give our total devotion . . . Jesus Christ, the Messiah, the Son of the Living God. True teaching always exalts Jesus Christ and honors Him. (John 16:13-14)

Deception, Delusion & Destruction

☑ 5. *There will often be an anti-Semitic smack to the false teacher's teaching.*

Before World War II, German Protestant leaders developed a theology which denied the Jewish origins of Christianity and wrote off the Jews as apostates who would never be saved. They considered Jews to be only good for the city dump ... a cursed people. As a result, by and large, German Protestantism accepted Adolf Hitler. The true Church could have stopped him, but do you know why they didn't? They were divided among themselves. Satan came in through deception and got them so confused about what was true and what was false that they were fighting each other. This left them powerless to stop the madman and the Holocaust that ensued.

There's a modern revival of Protestant Nazism going on today right here in the United States. There's anti-Semitism within segments of the Protestant church. It is not of God. Anti-Semitism is a foul deception. There are people who are saying that Israel is never going to be recognized by God as a nation. That's a lie from hell. Satan has always sought to eradicate the Jews. He hates Jesus Christ because Jesus exposed and smashed Satan's deceptive authority. The devil knows the Jews are going to be saved one day soon. He knows that the 144,000 that are spoken of in the book of Revelation are actually real Jews who will accept Jesus Christ; they'll go out and turn the world upside down for God. Satan will do anything to try to stop that. That's why there is anti-Semitism.

☑ 6. *They reject all authority.*

Jude says "They despise dominion." In the Greek language that means they reject authority. They don't want to be accountable to anyone.

Danger Signs

Satan's nature is that of rebellion. These deceivers are ministers of Satan, because, in nature, they are like their father — rebellious. God hates rebellion and rebellious spirits in any form.

> For rebellion is as the sin of witchcraft, and stubbornness is as iniquity and idolatry. Because thou hast rejected the word of the Lord, he hath also rejected thee from being king.
> —I Samuel 15:23

✓ 7. *They are often negative about revival and the wave of God's Spirit.*

Deceivers often prefer to be preachers of doom and destruction. You feel hopeless after hearing them or reading their literature. And for some reason, after hearing them your spirit is unsettled.

I don't know how many times doom has been prophesied to me. One guy walked up to me and said, "Oh, in the name of God, I prophesy over you. Thou shalt lead a great revival in the city of Lansing. Thy church shall grow to 50,000 and thou shalt lead the army of the Lord, saith God." Well, you know, it just didn't set right with me. I like it when people appreciate me. I'm like everybody else, I like to be appreciated. But when somebody tries to use the name of the Lord as a means of flattering me so they can get something from me, I get real agitated.

This particular man started prophesying falsely on a regular basis so I confronted him. I told him I thought his prophecies were from his own imagination, and I asked him to stop. Then he pronounced a prophecy of doom on me. He told me the church I pastored would cease to grow until only five people were left in the church. He prophesied total destruction for our church. I never saw him again.

Deception, Delusion & Destruction

Watch out for prophecies, messages of doom, and judgment predictions that leave deep agitation in the depths of your spirit. You'll lack a peace about these "words."

Listen to your heart. That's where God speaks to you. And stay close to His Word so you can side-step all religious deception.

We've discussed seven danger signs which point to possible deceivers. Keep these signs handy. You'll need them in the future as deception increases and Christ's return approaches.

Remember ...

☑ 1. The seven danger signs of deceivers.

    a) There is an exclusiveness about them.

    b) They generally major on minor issues rather than on the person and work of Jesus Christ.

    c) There seems to be an emphasis on extra Scriptural revelation, or a leader that has some divine inspiration that's equal to the Scriptures.

    d) There will be some strange twist about the teaching of Jesus Christ or the nature of God.

    e) There will often be an anti-Semitic smack to the false teacher's teaching.

    f) They reject all authority.

    g) They are often negative about revival and the wave of God's Spirit.

Chapter Nine:
The Delusion of Diversion

We're living in perilous times. These are dangerous times, but they're exciting times also.

Some time ago, one of our evangelists was traveling on an airplane. He happened to sit next to a woman who was fasting. When they brought lunch around she said, "No, I don't want any, I'm fasting." The evangelist said to her, "You must be a Christian." She responded "No I'm not a Christian! I'm a Satanist and we Satanists around the world are fasting and praying." The shocked evangelist asked, "What are you fasting and praying about?" She responded in a matter-of-fact manner, "We're fasting and praying to the devil that he will destroy every pastor in the world. We know that if we can tear down Christian leaders the sheep will scatter. The Church is becoming too strong and too big and has become a threat to us. We're going to do everything we can to tear it apart. And the way to do it is to destroy the pastor."

Well, if there had been just one report of this I would have a tendency to shrug it off as oratory

Deception, Delusion & Destruction

sensationalism, but the evangelist I mentioned has an exemplary reputation in a major denomination. In addition, one of our own missionaries, on a trip to Europe, ran into another person who was fasting and praying. He asked, "What are you fasting and praying about?" And this person said, "I'm a Satanist, and we're fasting and praying to the devil that he'll destroy every pastor and every church leader in the world. The church is becoming too strong and is a dangerous threat to us."

I believe we've come to that point in history when some will depart from the faith and others are going to get so turned on to Jesus there will be no stopping them. But it seems that the Satanist's strategy is working, at least in part. Last year, we lost some 20,000 ordained evangelical ministers who buckled under various pressures. What happened to their churches? What happened to their flocks? They have scattered.

I know a church that was bringing great damage to Satan's Kingdom in one particular city. When the Satanic onslaught came against the pastor, instead of getting behind him and praying for him, the people in that church were taking sides. They began to gossip and cause trouble. And do you know what has happened to that church? The pastor buckled under the pressure. He left the ministry and that church has become fragmented. That's the exact results these Satanists were looking for as they prayed and fasted to the devil.

I believe we're living in the hour of Revelation 12:12 when the devil knows he's got just a little time left. And so he's launching all out attacks against the Church of Jesus Christ, trying to fragment the church, tear it

The Delusion of Diversion

apart, and divert her energies into non-productive activities.

Yes, I believe one of the greatest deceptions in America, is the deception of diversion; getting church leaders off target from Christ's mandate.

Our mandate from God is threefold:

1. Worship of God (upward ministry)

2. Evangelization of the lost (outward ministry)

3. Building of believers (inward ministry)

All the church's money and resources, time and effort should be channeled into these three areas. Everything we do as Christians must have these objectives as our underlying mission.

For example, if we feed the hungry, it should be with the underlying goal of evangelizing them for Christ. If we have Bible studies, the essential goal should be to build believers into strong saints. Our music, our activities, our praise should be for the purpose of honoring and worshipping God, not just making ourselves feel good.

One of the devil's goals for the Church is DIVERSION. If, through deception, he can get the Church to swerve from it's real mission, he will then be safe to carry out his worldwide master plan of death and destruction. If the spiritual "Green Mamba" can deceive church leaders into devoting time, money and effort into special campaigns and crusades which have nothing to do with worship, evangelism, or building the saints, he can

Deception, Delusion & Destruction

successfully weaken the Church of her impact on the world.

The devil wants to confuse, divide, and frustrate the Church, giving him greater opportunities to carry on his end-time deception and destruction — unopposed by any unified spiritual effort.

People have asked me about a certain walk for the hungry campaign. "Why isn't your church involved?" Well the reason is because the money is not going to the hungry. It is going to a certain church council, and that council has been known to support anti-Israel activities, communist insurgencies, and prayer meetings with Buddhists, Hindus, and Muslims. They have supported Marxist regimes by purchasing arms, and have even provided pornography to many of their delegates during a convention. Do you think I want to walk for that?

I'm almost shaking on the inside right now when I think of the Christians who are being deceived. Deception! The devil tries to make these phoney fundraisers look like spiritual things. "Look at this! You are helping the hungry." My goodness! To be frank with you, our church gave more to the hungry, as an individual church, than all of those churches who participated in the so called "walk" put together. And we know that every penny went to the hungry for the goal of evangelization. It didn't go to support alcoholic drinks for delegates to the church council, or to provide them with pornography in their hotel rooms.

Some television programs which show little hungry children are good, but some are not. Some of them hire actors and actresses to raise money, and much of

The Delusion of Diversion

that money is actually going to other causes. I believe the devil is deceiving and diverting God's people's money into false projects. I get letters almost every day from overseas "projects" saying, "We want you to send us tape recorders, tapes, books and money." They send out these letters to sincere Christians. These unsuspecting, compassionate believers are in turn deceived into buying tape recorders, tapes, books and supplies and sending them to some unknown "church" or "missionary." And do you know what many of them are doing? They're selling these goods on the black market and then using the money for drugs, weapons, and other things. You could not believe what is going on in this world right now to divert God's money into false systems. It's awful!

We've discovered dozens of charlatans raising money for different types of projects and later found out they never even had a ministry. The F.B.I. called us one day about a con-man who was raising thousands of dollars from church people by making emergency appeals for mission funds.

And attempts are being made to divert more than just money. I believe the devil, through deception, is trying to divert the Christian's time. With all due respect, I think many Christians are spending too much time trying to make the ocean a better place for fish to live, when they should be trying to catch fish from the ocean. I'm constantly hearing people say, "You've got to be the salt." And then they'll pour on the pressure and guilt by saying something like, "If you don't picket the porno shop with us, then you're a lukewarm Christian. You've got to be the salt, you know . . . and . . . well . . . if you don't, then you're not being the salt!"

Deception, Delusion & Destruction

Well, as I understand salt, it's not something you do. Salt is something that you are or you aren't. It's like righteousness. It's not something you do. You either are or you aren't.

I know that when I'm worshipping God, winning souls, and building up believers then, as a natural result, I'll *be* the salt and the light God wants me to be. Fish will know they can come to my boat if they want to get out of the miserable mess they're trapped in. But rather than doing these things, many Christians are pouring their money into buying chemicals to dump into the ocean to make it a better place for the fish to live. Well those fish are pretty happy with the comfortable ocean now that Christians have invested all their time, effort and money into making it a better place for lost fish.

I believe the devil is also trying to divert the purpose of the Church. The purpose of the Church is to worship God, to train and equip believers for the work of the ministry, and to evangelize the lost. That is the purpose of the church.

Now, you'll find that when the church stays on target with its purpose something amazing happens: Revival comes! And when *revival* comes to the church there's a natural overflow. That overflow is called *reformation* of society.

The church can't reform society into revival. First the church must experience authentic revival and then the overflow of that revival becomes society's reform. And after society's reform, the church is, as a result, restored to her rightful position that God intended. But it starts with revival. If we try to use the political

The Delusion of Diversion

process, by carrying signs, criticizing and bellyaching, and "pouring chemicals into the ocean" to make this world a better place for those poor lost fish, do you know what we're going to do? We're going to lose all the way around because we've got the whole thing backwards.

Revival first. Then reformation, and finally restoration of the Church. But the revival has got to be first.

Deception. Oh how the enemy longs to get the church off target. What can you do to prevent deception and diversion in your life and in your church?

Ask questions: Are people being won to Jesus in my church? Do we really worship God in our church? Is the church building disciples for Jesus Christ? If you answer these questions with three "no's," something is amiss. Deception is somewhere.

Before giving to any political fund, do your research. Before getting involved in picketing, petition-signing, hunger campaigns, or missionary projects, ask questions. Any honest ministry will have a clear-cut mission statement. If they have integrity, they'll tell you exactly where the money is going, what the general expenses are, and a report of what percentage of the budget actually goes to the project.

As a Christian, you want to glorify God with your life. There's no better way to do that than by investing your time, money, and effort into things that are important to Him. Don't let a deceiver cheat you out of God's blessings. Work toward the goals that are important to God: Worship, evangelism, and building believers for Christ.

Deception, Delusion & Destruction

Give to projects which are endorsed by quality men of God who have proven their love for Christ and have lived lives of integrity. Always find out who endorses a project before getting involved. It's true. Satan is craving to pull God's servants off target. Pray for men and women of God. "Greater is He that is in you than he that is in the world." (I John 4:4)

Remember...

☑ 1. We are living in perilous times.

☑ 2. But these are exciting times.

☑ 3. Three areas of our God-given mandate:

   a) Worship God

   b) Evangelize the lost

   c) Build believers into disciples for Christ

☑ 4. Every project that looks good isn't.

☑ 5. Research any appeal for money from organizations or people you're unfamiliar with.

☑ 6. Don't fall for the deception of diversion.

Chapter Ten:
Who Tends to Follow the False?

I couldn't believe my eyes!

I had just visited a charismatic prayer meeting in a denominational church across town. There were only about twenty people there, but these twenty believers were genuinely enthusiastic about the things of God. We prayed, we worshipped, we studied the Bible together — it was all so refreshing.

But I was about to see something that would send shock waves down my spine. We concluded the prayer meeting and dismissed the participants to go home or to stay and fellowship with one another. Having a full schedule, I had to leave right away.

As I was leaving, I heard a loud commotion over in the fellowship hall. I thought maybe some more charismatic believers were in there getting excited about worshipping God exuberantly. So I thought I'd quietly walk through the hall on my way out. Now I wish I hadn't.

Deception, Delusion & Destruction

I opened the door of the church fellowship hall and suddenly, like a flash, I felt as though I had gone to hell. Smoke poured out of the room so thick, the hanging lights were having difficulty glowing through the tobacco clouds. The smell of alcohol was in the air, mixed with the smoke — it was a smell like that of an old bowling alley.

People, perhaps 200 or more, were sitting around tables, cursing, swearing, placing their chips and marks on their gambling cards. A moderator hollered over the microphone, "B-15!" "G-88." I was numb with the jolt of what I saw and heard. I can't explain what I felt. It was anger, mixed with fear, coupled with disappointment, pity, and disgrace. I was ashamed and hurt for Jesus. I felt what He must have been feeling. I don't think I could have been more heavy-hearted or grieved if I had walked into Sodom and Gomorrah. It was horrible.

I ran out of that place like an olympic sprinter. I could take no more of this debauchery in a building they called "God's house."

To me, the whole thing was a mockery of God's love and grace. But, I couldn't be too harsh. You see, I knew those people in the "gambling hall" of the church had been deceived by spiritual leaders who were preaching a "different gospel" and a "different Jesus."

Not all gospels are the same. Not all Jesuses are the same. Sounds incredible, doesn't it? But look at what St. Paul said when he was addressing some gullible people:

Who Tends to Follow the False?

> You seem so gullible: you believe whatever anyone tells you even if he is preaching about another Jesus than the one we preach, or a different spirit than the Holy Spirit you received, or shows you a different way to be saved. You swallow it all.
> — II Corinthians 11:4 (TLB)

Notice, there is "another Jesus" and a "different spirit." People who do not rely daily on God's Word — the Bible — may actually be following the wrong Jesus or listening to the wrong spirit.

"A CURSE ON THOSE WHO PREACH 'ANOTHER GOSPEL'."

Paul pronounced a curse on anyone who would preach a different gospel than the gospel presented clearly in the Scriptures. The believers in Galatia received the true gospel, but soon turned after a different "gospel." Look what St. Paul said:

> I marvel that ye are so soon removed from him that called you into the grace of Christ unto another gospel: Which is not another; but there be some that trouble you, and would pervert the gospel of Christ. But though we, or an angel from heaven, preach any other gospel unto you than that which we have preached unto you, let him be accursed.
> — Galatians 1:6-8

Paul says that other gospels are "perverted" in some way. The spiritual leaders of the church with the gambling hall, have perverted the gospel of Christ. They are false prophets, leading hundreds on the road to a devastating conclusion.

Deception, Delusion & Destruction

Other gospels teach licentiousness and call it "Christian liberty." Or they teach legalism and call it "holiness." They may teach that there are mediators between God and man, besides Jesus Christ. This is a perversion of the gospel, thus it becomes "another gospel." They may say you are saved by grace, but kept in God's family by your work for Him. This, too, is a perversion of the true gospel.

Years ago, as a young Christian, I was walking in the grace of God and loving it. I enjoyed being saved (I still do!). I always maintained a cheerful attitude, but one day an older Christian man walked up to me with his head cocked sideways and looking at me out of the corner of his eyes, he said with a deep spiritual tone, "You're happy and joyful now, and that's fine. But don't get your hope and faith up too high, because tomorrow you may fall flat on your face and be lost from God's presence. How can you ever know what tomorrow will bring? You may lose it all."

It took me back for a minute, then I remembered the verse to a great song, Amazing Grace. I smiled and responded respectfully to the older gentleman,

"... 'Twas grace that brought me safe this far and grace will lead me home."

Oh, the grace of God! I love the song called "I've Been Sealed."

> I've been sealed by the Holy Spirit
> Saved by grace, and I want you to hear it
> Born again, I've got nothing to fear
> So I'll smile, and shed a thankful tear.

Who Tends to Follow the False?

>Ain't nobody gonna take my joy away
>Ain't no teacher gonna be teachin' me astray
>I've been washed in the Blood
>And I know I'm here to stay
>Hey, hey, hey
>So I'll get on my knees
>And thank the Lord while I pray.

The joy and security of walking closely with Jesus is so precious. Why trade it for a false teaching that will bring you into a tangled up bondage and that will steal your peace and joy and faith?

WHO IS SUSCEPTIBLE TO THE "DIFFERENT GOSPELS"?

I've found six classes of individuals who seem to walk from one false concept to another. My prayer is that they'll find out before it's too late.

☑ 1. *Those led by their sinful lusts.*

>Having a form of godliness, but denying the power thereof: from such turn away. For of this sort are they which creep into houses, and lead captive silly women laden with sins, led away with divers lusts, ever learning, and never able to come to the knowledge of the truth.
>
>— II Timothy 3:5-7

☑ 2. *Adulterers, either spiritual or physical.*

>But whoso committeth adultery with a woman lacketh understanding: he that doeth it destroyeth his own soul.
>
>— Proverbs 6:32

Deception, Delusion & Destruction

☑ 3. *Those who aren't satisfied with simple Bible Truths.*

He answered and said unto them, When it is evening, ye say, It will be fair weather: for the sky is red. And in the morning, It will be foul weather to day: for the sky is red and lowering. O ye hypocrites, ye can discern the face of the sky; but can ye not discern the signs of the times? A wicked and adulterous generation seeketh after a sign; and there shall no sign be given unto it, but the sign of the prophet Jonas. And he left them, and departed.
— Matthew 16:2-4

☑ 4. *Those who think more about things from a human standpoint than from God's standpoint.*

Jesus turned to Peter and said, "Get away from me, you Satan! You are a dangerous trap to me. You are thinking merely from a human point of view, and not from God's."

— Matthew 16:23 (TLB)

☑ 5. *Those living carelessly or being preoccupied with problems and cares.*

And take heed to yourselves, lest at any time your hearts be overcharged with surfeiting, and drunkenness, and cares of this life, and so that day come upon you unawares. For as a snare shall it come on all them that dwell on the face of the whole earth. Watch ye therefore, and pray always, that ye may be accounted worthy to escape all these things that shall come to pass, and to stand before the Son of man.

— Luke 21:34-36

Who Tends to Follow the False?

☑ 6. *The Self-righteous.*

And he spake this parable unto certain which trusted in themselves that they were righteous, and despised others.

— Luke 18:9

As it is written, There is none righteous, no, not one.

— Romans 3:10

But we are all as an unclean thing, and all our righteousnesses are as filthy rags; and we all do fade as a leaf; and our iniquities, like the wind, have taken us away.

— Isaiah 64:6

WHAT YOU CAN DO

You may ask, "What can I do to protect myself?" Simple. Read and study the Bible yourself. Don't depend on someone else to keep you safe.

Secondly, get into a church that is "turned-on" for Jesus Christ. Listen to pastors who teach from the Bible. Get plugged in to a ministry in the church and begin to reach out to others. Find your place in a local church.

Finally, determine to mature in Christ. You can only do that through praying, reading the Bible, fellowshipping with other believers, and reaching out to others.

When Jude wrote his epistle, he was probably concerned about the readers. After all, he had just written a letter of warning about false prophets, deception, and delusion. His readers probably wondered how

Deception, Delusion & Destruction

they could keep from falling. So Jude concluded his letter this way:

> Now unto him that is able to keep you from falling, and to present you faultless before the presence of his glory with exceeding joy, To the only wise God our Saviour, be glory and majesty, dominion and power, both now and ever. Amen.
> — Jude 24-25

The Lord can keep you from falling into any deception. Get close to Him.

Remember ...

☑ 1. Not all "gospels" are the same.

☑ 2. Not all "Jesuses" are genuine.

Only one is the Way, the Truth, and the Life. Only one can get you into heaven.

☑ 3. Six classes of people who are prone to follow perverted gospels:

a) Those led by their sinful lusts.

b) Adulterers, either spiritual or physical.

c) Those who aren't satisfied with simple Bible Truths.

d) Those who think more about things from a human standpoint than from God's standpoint.

Who Tends to Follow the False?

- e) Those living carelessly or being preoccupied with problems and cares.

- f) The Self-righteous.

☑ 4. Remember, the Lord can . . . and will . . . keep you from falling into deception if you'll draw close to Him.

Chapter Eleven:
On the Thin Edge of Disaster

Deception is a clear characteristic of the predicted coming apostasy.

> And with all deceivableness of unrighteousness in them that perish; because they received not the love of the truth, that they might be saved.
> — II Thessalonians 2:10

Many people are living on the thin edge of disaster as a result of the rampant deception that is flooding our world today. The deceptive allurements are all around us. The soul's enemy is propping up more enticements than ever before, hoping to allure many from Christ and toward some cheap scheme. His goal is to ensnare and enslave. Satan is a merciless, enslaving dictator.

> . . . Appealing to the lustful desires of sinful human nature, they entice people who are just escaping from those who live in error. They promise them freedom, while they themselves are slaves of depravity — for a man is a slave to whatever has mastered him.
> — II Peter 2:18-19 (NIV)

Deception, Delusion & Destruction

I read an article some time ago in the Fort Lauderdale *News & Sun Sentinel*. The sub-headlines read, "Bright Lights Lure Turtles to Death." The article told about more than 200 newly hatched sea turtles that were dazed by bright street lights. By instinct, when sea turtles hatch they move toward the reflection of the moon on the ocean. These turtles thought they were heading for the water, but instead they made their way toward the busy highway and catastrophe.

I wonder how many people have gone toward the "wrong light," only to find themselves hopelessly crushed in the end? How many have walked after illusions rather than reality? Actor Gregory Harrison, in an Associated Press release, told his story of how he was following an enslaving illusion:

> ... Harrison went through more than $700,000 worth of cocaine before he realized he was "sitting in the back seat of my addiction and the devil was driving." Harrison, who played Dr. Gonzo Gates on the television show Trapper John, M.D., has a new role as spokesman for the Entertainment Industry Referral and Assistance Center. The Los Angeles center has helped about 3,000 industry workers seeking treatment for substance abuse. Harrison said of his early drug use, "It's very insidious. It lets you get away with it just enough times to be convinced you will always get away with it. I felt more intelligent, more handsome, more creative, witty and charming. My acting didn't suffer for a long time. It's that convincing an illusion."

Satan is the master of illusion.

Deception and cult crime has become so bad in America that there is now an official cult awareness

On the Thin Edge of Disaster

network operating in 40 of the 50 states. In addition, a national organization of police officers has formed a CULT CRIME IMPACT NETWORK (CCIN). They deal in investigating crimes of the occult.

My ten-year old daughter came home from school one day quite upset. Her teacher told the class that witchcraft was the force that landed her a teaching job. A little girl perked up when the teacher gave the class that tidbit of information and proudly announced, "My mother practices witchcraft too. She knows how to put spells on people."

Satan desires to operate through the human mind. And he has little trouble infiltrating and outwitting the intellectual, carnal mind. But, thank God, Satan is no match for the mind and power of Christ.

Still, tens of thousands annually are lured into deception which costs them their lives... and worse yet ... their eternity. One leading authority reports that between 40,000 and 60,000 people are murdered in Satanic rituals each year. The people who join these satanic cults have the hopes of gaining power and privilege beyond anything they ever imagined. But what they don't know is that disaster awaits them. They're walking into a trap that's waiting to be suddenly sprung.

We received horrifying reports of the mass slayings of teenagers in Brownsville, Texas, and Matamoros, Mexico. What provoked these bloody murders? Cultists, appealing to Satan for protection, offered innocent victims as sacrifices. One spokesman said, "Satan is demanding more and more today."

Deception, Delusion & Destruction

ABOMINABLE PRACTICES TODAY

There are many practices today that are deceiving people to walk on the edge of disaster and destruction. Let's take a look at some of them.

> There shall not be found among you any one that maketh his son or his daughter to pass through the fire, or that useth divination, or an observer of times, or an enchanter, or a witch, or a charmer or a consulter with familiar spirits, or a wizard, or a necromancer. For all that do these things are an abomination unto the Lord: and because of these abominations the Lord thy God doth drive them out from before thee. Thou shalt be perfect with the Lord thy God.
>
> But the prophet, which shall presume to speak a word in my name, which I have not commanded him to speak, or that shall speak in the name of other gods, even that prophet shall die. And if thou say in thine heart, "How shall we know the word which the Lord hath not spoken?" When a prophet speaketh in the name of the Lord, if the thing follow not, nor come to pass, that is the thing which the Lord hath not spoken, but the prophet hath spoken it presumptuously: thou shalt not be afraid of him.
> — Deuteronomy 18:10-13, 20-22

№ 1 — CHILD SACRIFICE (see verse 10)

Today this would be called "abortion." Satan is a child molester, abuser, and murderer.

№ 2 — DIVINATION (verse 10)

This can be any practice that charms a victim until their mental control is in the hands of an outside force.

On the Thin Edge of Disaster

№ 3 — OBSERVER OF TIMES (verse 10)

This is dabbling into horoscopes — astrology. Today, Americans can dial a telephone number daily to receive their current horoscope. What a shock it was to learn that the wife of one of our great American presidents regularly consulted an astrologer.

> And lest thou lift up thine eyes unto heaven, and when thou seest the sun, and the moon, and the stars, even all the host of heaven, shouldest be driven to worship them, and serve them, which the Lord thy God hath divided unto all nations under the whole heaven.
>
> — Deuteronomy 4:19

> Stand now with thine enchantments, and with the multitude of thy sorceries, wherein thou hast labored from thy youth; if so be thou shalt be able to profit, if so be thou mayest prevail. Thou art wearied in the multitude of thy counsels. Let now the astrologers, the stargazers, the monthly prognosticators, stand up, and save thee from these things that shall come upon thee. Behold, they shall be as stubble; the fire shall burn them; they shall not deliver themselves from the power of the flame: there shall not be a coal to warm at, nor fire to sit before it.
>
> — Isaiah 47:12-14

№ 4 — ENCHANTMENTS (verse 10)

This involves any of the following:

a) Voodoo
b) Black magic
c) Spells, hexes, curses
d) Enchanting drugs (marijuana, cocaine, etc.)

Deception, Delusion & Destruction

Nº 5 — WITCHCRAFT (verse 10)

It speaks of witches and wizards. This involves the whole spectrum of white magic, black magic, and general witchcraft (which is earth worship).

Nº 6 — CHARMER (verse 11)

A charmer is one who uses chants or trinkets to try to bring about a desired effect. This includes, but is not limited to:

a) healing crystals
b) hypnosis
c) pendulum healers

Nº 7 — CONSULTER OF FAMILIAR SPIRITS (verse 11)

This is a "medium" who may conduct seances to contact the dead. It includes "channeler," seeking to get in touch with "spirit guides".

Nº 8 — NECROMANCY (verse 11)

This is another forbidden practice which is simply the attempting to speak to or contact the dead in any way. Yes, even praying to dead saints is a form of necromancy. An interesting article in USA TODAY said that 42 percent of American people believe they've had contact with the dead. This is a form of the forbidden, deceptive practice of necromancy.

Moses lists these practices as abominations — things God hates. Why does he especially hate these practices? I believe it's because they deceive people into

On the Thin Edge of Disaster

trusting Satan — although ignorantly — instead of trusting the true, loving God through Jesus Christ.

In countless ways Americans are being deceived by drinking in Eastern philosophies about the power of the mind. His goal is to plant seeds that will eventually bear bitter fruit.

Truth is narrow. Deception and falsehood is wide. For example there is only one right answer for two plus two. Answer: four. There are unlimited wrong answers.

There is one true light. All others are impostors. There is one genuine Christ. All others are frauds. There is one way to heaven. All other ways are deceptions.

If you are a Christian today, I have wonderful news for you. That's this: There is not one promise of defeat for you in God's word. Every promise for the child of God is a promise of victory. If we are walking with Christ, in Him we have victory over sin, temptation, and deception.

> . . . In all these things we are more than conquerors through Him that loved us.
> —Romans 8:37

> Submit yourselves therefore to God. Resist the devil, and he will flee from you.
> —James 4:7

> Behold, I give unto you power to tread on serpents and scorpions, and over all the power of the enemy: and nothing shall by any means hurt you.
> —Luke 10:19

Deception, Delusion & Destruction

> Ye are of God, little children, and have overcome them: because greater is He that is in you, than he that is in the world.
> — I John 4:4

How much power of deception does Satan have over our lives? None! If we will live, and move, and have our life hidden in Christ Jesus, we have the power over Satan's deceptions.

Remember ...

☑ 1. Bright lights lure turtles to death.

☑ 2. Satan provides illusions; Jesus gives reality.

☑ 3. Satan can only infiltrate the carnal mind.

☑ 4. Abominable practices:

   a) Child Sacrifice
   b) Divination
   c) Observer of Times
   d) Enchantments
   e) Witchcraft
   f) Charmer
   g) Consulter of Familiar Spirits
   h) Necromancy

☑ 5. Truth is narrow. Deception and falsehood is broad.

☑ 6. Satan has no power of deception over the child of God who is submitted to Christ.

Chapter Twelve:
Our Divine Defense Against Deception

Jesus warned us that deception would grow, intensely and become more dangerous as we near His Return. (Matthew 24:4,5,11,24; Mark 13:5,6; Luke 21:8) Paul warned us as well.

> But evil men and seducers shall wax worse and worse, deceiving, and being deceived.
> — II Timothy 3:13

During World War II, enemies of the United States would carefully paint aerial pictures of airports on open fields in hopes of deceiving the American bombers. The bomber squadrons would see what appeared to be an enemy air field and waste their bomb power attacking empty fields.

DECEPTION!

I remember a certain false prophet in the sixties and early seventies who had entire congregations convinced that charismatics were witches invading the earth. Churches began to stock guns and ammunition

Deception, Delusion & Destruction

in order to protect themselves from these "witches." Oh, what heartache, embarrassment, shame and loss came to those undiscerning churches who diverted their energies from preaching the gospel to preparing for war with fellow brothers and sisters in Christ.

God has not left the Church defenseless against such deception. He's given us a powerful tool — a gift — to be developed and used in protecting the Church from impostors. We have a spiritual "sonar" called "discerning of spirits."

> To another the working of miracles; to another prophecy; to another discerning of spirits; to another divers kinds of tongues; to another the interpretation of tongues.
> — I Corinthians 12:10

The spirit world is real. The danger of deceiving spirits is increasing daily. This supernatural gift of discerning of spirits is like our immune system. It will protect the Church from "foreign substance" and keep her well, even in times of great danger.

Each passing day the danger of encounters with deceiving spirits is increasing. Jesus told us that as we near the culmination of time, many false prophets will arise on the world scene.

Even in many Christian circles, we are witnessing the introduction of a new subjectiveness. Some Christians are becoming more experience-oriented and less Word-of-God-oriented. This can be dangerous. False prophets and false teachers are lurking, many of them around the body of Christ — the Church — waiting to secretly introduce damnable heresies (II Peter 2:1-3; Acts 20:28-31).

Our Divine Defense Against Deception

But God did not leave His Church defenseless! He has provided a spiritual sonar: the gift of discerning of spirits.

What Is This Gift?

It is not:

1. The "gift" of suspicion
2. The "gift" of fault finding
3. Natural insight
4. Intellectual discernment
5. Discerning of demons

It is:

Discerning of spirits! By definition the Greek declares that this gift is "a piercing of all that is outward and seeing right through to the spirit of the matter."

This gift allows a person to see the real motivating forces behind:

1. People
2. Doctrines
3. Supernatural-type manifestations

The Purpose of This Gift

The gift of discerning of spirits provides a person with a means of "seeing" right into the spirit realm to determine what spirit is motivating a person, doctrine, or action. A person with this gift clearly knows whether the motivating spirit is the Holy Spirit, the human spirit, or an evil spirit.

Defensively, this gift protects the Church from impostors. Offensively, it provides revelation knowledge helpful in casting out demon spirits.

People in the Bible
Who Have Discerned the Lord

1. Moses
2. Abraham
3. Stephen while being stoned to death
4. Paul on the Damascus Road

People in the Bible
Who Have Discerned Angels

1. Joshua
2. Gideon
3. Daniel
4. Mary
5. The Apostles (Acts 5:19)
6. Peter (Acts 12)
7. Philip (Acts 8)

People in the Bible
Who Have Discerned the
Condition of the Human Heart

1. Jesus (John 1:47-50)
2. Peter discerned Ananias & Sapphira's hearts (Acts 5)
3. Peter discerned Simon's false motives (Acts 8)

People in the Bible
Who Have Discerned Evil Spirits

1. Jesus (Matthew 16)

Our Divine Defense Against Deception

2. Paul (Acts 16). The demon-possessed girl was saying all the right things, but it was a demon motivating her. It's possible to say the right things in the wrong spirit.

Evil spirits can hinder a nation. They can hinder a church, a family, a business. That's why they must be identified and cast out!

Every pastor needs to pray that God will use him in discerning of spirits. Churches would be saved from much agony and pain if pastors would listen to that acute agitation that flares up on the inside of them when they meet certain individuals.

I remember a certain individual who was in a church leadership position when I accepted the new pastorate. For some reason I had a bad feeling about this fellow. I didn't like being around him. I almost became nauseated just shaking his hand. What was wrong? I found myself repenting for feeling this way when God gently spoke to my heart about His gift of discerning of spirits. So I acted on it and removed this man from his visible leadership position.

I was accused of being "unloving," "dictatorial," and even worse. Nonetheless, I stuck to my decision. A month or so later this man's hypocrisy was exposed. He was secretly committing some of the most disgusting sins you could imagine. Thank God, I had removed him from leadership before his horrible sins became public. The church was spared public embarrassment.

On another occasion a singing evangelist kept calling and asking me to book him in church. There was that agitation in my spirit again. I kept telling him

Deception, Delusion & Destruction

"no." He persisted, almost to the point where he was irritating me, but again, I stuck to my decision. I understand that I was severely criticized by this fellow in a number of ways.

Well, a few months went by and he was exposed! He was in dreadful sin, enjoying it, and still "ministering in song" where undiscerning pastors would permit him in their pulpits. I don't want our church exposed to this type of hypocritical ministry.

We need to listen to the gift of discerning of spirits.

It's true. Deception is in the world. It seems easier to find than reality. But God has given the believer everything he needs to discern deception, expose it, and turn people from it.

As we walk in the Spirit, with Jesus Christ as Lord, we'll avoid the coming deception, delusion, and destruction.

> Ye are of God, little children, and have overcome them: because greater is He that is in you, than he that is in the world.
>
> — I John 4:4

Recommended Reading

Bob Larson. *Larson's Book of Cults*. Tyndale House Publishers, 1982.

Josh McDowell and Don Stewart. *Handbook of Today's Religions*. Here's Life Publishers, 1983.

Erwin W. Lutzer and John F. DeVries. *Satan's Evangelistic Strategy for this New Age*. Victor Books, SP Publications, Inc., 1989.

Hal Lindsey. *Combat Faith*. Bantam Books, 1986.

Richard W. DeHaan. *Satan, Satanism and Witchcraft*. Zondervan Corporation, 1972.

Raphael Gasson. *The Challenging Counterfeit*. Logos Books, 1966.

Maurice C. Burrell and J. Stafford Wright. *Whom Then Can We Believe?* Moody Press, 1978.

Richard Mayhue. *Unmasking Satan*. Victor Books, 1988.

Dan Peters, Steve Peters, and Cher Merrill. *What About Christian Rock?* Bethany House Publishers, 1986.

Norman Geisler. *False Gods of Our Time*. Harvest House Publishers, 1985.

Lester Sumrall. *Supernatural Principalities and Powers*. Thomas Nelson Publishers, 1983.

Lester Sumrall. *Alien Entities*. Harrison House, 1984.

ABOUT THE AUTHOR

Dave Williams is pastor of Mount Hope Church and International Outreach Ministries with over 4000 regular attenders. On the ministry's scenic 43 acres sits the new multi-million dollar worship and teaching center, designed to comfortably seat over 3000 people. The new complex includes educational facilities, executive offices, a television production center, and world outreach headquarters.

Williams is president of Mount Hope Bible Training Institute, author of 72 audio cassette teaching programs, two leadership video training programs, and has written 27 books, including the seven-time best seller, *The Start of Something Wonderful*. His written articles and reviews have appeared in newspapers and magazines nationwide.

Dave is seen weekly on the television programs, DAVE WILLIAMS AND MOUNT HOPE ALIVE and THE PACESETTER'S PATH. His international speaking ministry has taken him to several nations including parts of Europe, Tanzania, South Africa, and other places of the world.

Dave resides in the Lansing area with his wife, Mary Jo, and their children.

For a complete catalog of books, tapes, videos, and courses by Dave Williams, write to:

Dave Williams
202 South Creyts Road
Lansing, MI 48917

Please include your prayer requests and comments when you write.

More FAITHBUILDING BOOKS
by Dave Williams

THE SECRET OF POWER WITH GOD

Here are thirty chapters filled with concise information about prayer that brings results. You'll learn proper prayer management, God's address, the miracle of thanksgiving, how to discern God's will, and "tons" of other helpful "secrets" of power with God.

0-938020-15-3 .... $2.95

THE DESIRES OF YOUR HEART ...
... CAN BECOME REALITIES!

How to Change Your Dreams Into Realities; How to Develop Faith That Works; How to Receive Heaven-sent Ideas; How to Win When Facing Opposition; 15 Causes of Failure and How to Avoid Them; Setting and Reaching Your Goals. 149 pages of practical faith-building material!

0-938020-02-1 .... $2.95

THE CHRISTIAN
JOB-HUNTER'S HANDBOOK

101 pages of practical help for finding the right job — even in a recession! You'll learn how to prepare an effective resume, how to find your calling in life, and how to get the job you want!

0-938020-01-3 .... $3.25

THE NEW LIFE ...
THE START OF SOMETHING WONDERFUL

Our best seller! This book is being used by pastors, evangelists, teachers, and missionaries in many parts of the world. 44 pages of practical, concise guidelines to experiencing a victorious walk with Jesus Christ. The perfect book to give to new convert. QUANTITY PRICES AVAILABLE.

0-938020-03-X $1.95
0-938020-21-8 (Spanish Edition) $1.95

BESTSELLER

SUCCESS PRINCIPLES
FROM THE LIPS OF JESUS

In this book, Dave Williams shares 10 powerful principles for success in your life. You'll learn how to follow God's guidance, overcome procrastination, accomplish more, and become the pacesetter God wants you to be.

0-938020-00-5 .... $2.95

■ Quantity Discounts Available ■
MOUNT HOPE PUBLICATIONS
202 S. Creyts Rd. ■ Lansing, MI 48917

More FAITHBUILDING BOOKS
by Dave Williams

THE ART OF PACESETTING LEADERSHIP

Are you the kind of leader God is looking for? Find out by reading The Art of Pacesetting Leadership—an entire Leadership & Ministry Development course in itself. Taken from Pastor Dave's highly acclaimed "Pacesetting Leadership" class, this book's topics include: Levels of Leadership, Qualities Exhibited in Master-Level Leaders, The Kind of Leader God is Looking For, How to Overcome Stress and Pressure in the Ministry, and so much more. This is perhaps Pastor Williams' most important book.

0-938020-34-X $7.95

THE PASTOR'S PAY

Most church members have little or no knowledge of the concerns, frustrations, and needs of their pastor. Dave Williams, in a gentle, tender way, takes a close look at how much a pastor is worth, who sets his pay, and the scriptural guidelines for paying him. You'll learn the Biblical principles for setting the pastor's pay.

0-938020-36-6 .... $4.95

SLAIN IN THE SPIRIT IS IT REAL OR FAKE?

What would you think if you saw someone fall, as if dead, to the ground? What if the fall accompanied foaming at the mouth? . . . moaning and groaning? Is it real? Is it fake? This book explains Satanic Manifestations versus God's Visitations, The Supernatural Power and Manifestations of God's Glory, The Purpose of Signs and Wonders, Abuses and Shams, The History of This Phenomenon, Why Some Oppose This Manifestation, and When Does Being Slain in the Spirit Occur.

0-938020-32-3 .... $1.50

GETTING TO KNOW YOUR HEAVENLY FATHER

This book will lead you into that personal relationship with your heavenly Father you so desire. It discusses Christianity as a wonderful and fulfilling family relationship, not merely a religious experience. Find out the difference between theological tradition and the truth of God's character. Also included are Principles For Parents, and How to Claim Your Daily Benefits As a Child of God.

0-938020-35-8 .... $1.50

15 BIG CAUSES OF FAILURE

God did not create you to fail. He created you to succeed and have victory in every area of your life. This Mount Hope micro-book book takes a look at 15 common causes of failure in believer's lives and how to avoid them. You'll also learn how to get on that road to success which God has ordained for your life.

0-938020-13-7 .... $1.00

• Quantity Discounts Available •
MOUNT HOPE PUBLICATIONS
202 S. Creyts Rd. • Lansing, MI 48917

More FAITHBUILDING BOOKS
by Dave Williams

LONELY IN THE MIDST OF A CROWD

Did you know that severe loneliness can cause severe health problems? Some escape routes lead nowhere, but this book by Dave Williams shows the simple two-fold answer to loneliness. You never need to be lonely again.

0-938020-26-9 .... $1.25

7 SIGNPOSTS ON THE ROAD TO SPIRITUAL MATURITY

Are you maturing spiritually, or have you stalled in your walk with God? This book points out seven sure-fire indicators of spiritual maturity. Learn where you stand now, and where you need to go in order to experience the benefits of a spiritually mature life.

0-938020-29-3 .... $1.50

UNDERSTANDING SPIRITUAL GIFTS

Dave Williams says, "There is no resting point spiritually. We must keep growing and reaching for all that God has for us, or else spiritual paralysis will set in." In this book, an excerpt from *Finding Your Ministry and Gifts*, Pastor Williams concisely explains each spiritual gift and how to function properly in it. A much-needed book for Charismatics and Pentecostals. 32 pages.

0-938020-31-5 .... $1.75

THE REVIVAL POWER OF MUSIC

Does music bring in the glory of God? Dave Williams tells how the tremendous power of God can be released when the song of the Lord comes to His people's hearts. He'll take you on a journey in history, studying great revivals, and how music accompanied them. Does music take commitment? Is it a cure for depression? . . . A deliverance from oppression? Learn what the to hindrances to praise and worship are, and how music can bring victory. A Mount Hope micro-book.

0-938020-33-1 .... $1.00

TONGUES AND INTERPRETATION

How would you like to be charged-up with supernatural power from God? You can learn the secret of using your prayer language daily. This micro-book discusses the baptism in the Holy Spirit, the supernatural language, and how you, as a believer, can interpret your supernatural language of the Spirit. Learn the history of speaking in tongues in the Christian church. What did Augustine, Martin Luther, and others say about tongues? Find out, as you read this Mount Hope micro-book, "Tongues and Interpretation."

0-938020-37-4 .... $1.00

• Quantity Discounts Available •
MOUNT HOPE PUBLICATIONS
202 S. Creyts Rd. • Lansing, MI 48917

More FAITHBUILDING BOOKS by Dave Williams

THE AIDS PLAGUE

How does the AIDS crisis affect you? Believe it or not, before long everyone will be affected in some way or another by the tragedy of this deadly virus. Is there any hope? YES! In this book, Dave Williams gives you the answer to the AIDS crisis and tells how you can be protected.

0-938020-38-2 .... $1.95

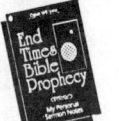

END-TIMES BIBLE PROPHECY —
My Personal Sermon Notes

These are Dave Williams' actual sermon notes from an extended series on Bible prophecy. In a concise form, you can now study events that will affect you: The Rapture • The Great Tribulation • The Coming of Antichrist ... and much more.

0-938020-39-0 .... $1.75

THE SUPERNATURAL GIFTS
OF THE HOLY SPIRIT — My Personal Sermon Notes

What a terrific reference resource. Students, teachers, preachers, anybody can benefit from these actual notes from Dave Williams' sermons on spiritual gifts. These compact, practical outlined notes on the Gifts of the Holy Spirit will help you to study like never before.

0-938020-40-4 .... $1.75

SUPERNATURAL SOULWINNING

Something big is happening! God has given us just a little more time to participate in His end-time revival. That means you and I have the chance to see this revival explode into the greatest, most successful harvest before the Church blasts off from this earth in a cloud of glory and splendor. How can we reach so many people if time is so short? How can we see our loved ones, our neighbors, our co-workers saved? These are questions Pastor Dave brought to the Lord in urgent prayer. In Supernatural Soulwinning, Dave Williams shares the simple plan God gave him for this enormous end-time revival.

0-938020-41-2 .... $1.95

SOMEBODY OUT THERE NEEDS YOU!

But I'm no evangelist," you say? That may be true. Your gift may not be that of an evangelist, but that doesn't exclude you from being a soulwinner. Along with salvation comes the great privilege of spreading the gospel. And that doesn't need to be burdensome; it's the mistakes we make while trying to witness that discourage us and make evangelism seem like a hard task. Learning how to avoid these 12 common mistakes will help you evangelize your friends, neighbors and loved ones.

0-938020-42-0 .... $1.75

• Quantity Discounts Available •
MOUNT HOPE PUBLICATIONS
202 S. Creyts Rd. • Lansing, MI 48917

More FAITHBUILDING BOOKS
by Dave Williams

REMEDY FOR WORRY AND TENSION

Are you bored with life? Do you feel tired... run down? If so, you may be suffering from the deadly disease of worry! In this book, Dave Williams shows how you can break loose from the pollution of worry and tension!

0-938020-27-7 .... $1.25

FINDING YOUR MINISTRY AND GIFTS

Find out where you fit in! At last... a concise, point-by-point study book defining and describing the ministries and gifts from God. You'll study: personality gifts, charismatic gifts, ministry gifts, supportive gifts, plus much, much more.

0-938020-16-8 .... $5.95

THE GRAND FINALE:
A STUDY ON THE COMING END-TIME REVIVAL

What does the future hold? Will it be revival? Dave Williams says "YES!" This book takes you on a journey into the very near future and describes some of the exciting events just ahead for the Church of Jesus Christ. Find out: How to prepare for the coming revival; What the latter rain will bring; Conditions for revival.

0-938020-18-8 .... $1.75

THE MINISTRY OF
LAYING ON OF HANDS

A guide into a fundamental Bible doctrine. Learn about: imparting blessings, transmitting God's power, administering the Holy Spirit Baptism, revealing or confirming spiritual gifts, and the abuses of this ministry. Dave Williams examines the Bible's answer to this often misunderstood doctrine.

0-938020-23-4 .... $1.75

PATIENT DETERMINATION

Is the Christian life worth all the trouble? Why are there so many problems along the way? *Patient Determination* presents Bible-truths for turning setbacks into victories.

0-938020-24-2 .... $1.00

• Quantity Discounts Available •
MOUNT HOPE PUBLICATIONS
202 S. Creyts Rd. • Lansing, MI 48917

More FAITHBUILDING BOOKS by Dave Williams

FAITH GOALS... THE SECRET OF SETTING AND REACHING THEM

Find out how you can become a peak achiever for God. This book describes how to make plans, set goals and get results. Did you know that only about 5% of all people in America have specific goals, and those who do will achieve 100 to 1000 times more in their lifetime? Faith Goals is an 8-1/2 X 11 inch book, complete with worksheets!

0-938020-04-8 .... $3.95

GENUINE PROSPERITY... A BIBLICAL PERSPECTIVE

High utility bills? Inflation? Rising food costs? If these concern you and your family, you need this book. Dave Williams shares the simple, Scriptural way to get out of debt, clean up your finances, and climb onto the road to complete financial victory.

0-938020-10-2 .... $1.25

HOW TO GET OUT OF THE TORMENTING CAVE OF DEPRESSION

This micro-book describes in detail what it's like to be depressed, symptoms of depression, its effects, how to recognize the roots of depression, etc. This anointed teaching will show the depressed person how to get out of the tormenting cave of depression, and climb to the peak of "victory mountain."

0-983020-25-0 .... $1.50

GROWING UP IN OUR FATHER'S FAMILY

Learn the Kingdom Keys to Growing up spiritually. You'll study the babyhood, childhood, and mature stages of spiritual growth (Which one are you in?), discover the "master key" to greatness, and discover the amazing benefits of practicing the "extra-miler" principle.

0-938020-11-0 .... $1.25

THE BEAUTY OF HOLINESS

This easily-read book delves into the often ignored and seldom understood topic of holiness. Practical and concise, it teaches what holiness is and what it is not, the advantages of holy living, and how you can follow holiness.

0-938020-22-6 .... $1.25

• Quantity Discounts Available •
MOUNT HOPE PUBLICATIONS
202 S. Creyts Rd. • Lansing, MI 48917

More FAITHBUILDING BOOKS
by Dave Williams

DECEPTION, DELUSION & DESTRUCTION

Someone wants desperately to deceive you . . . but you can crush any attempt toward your destruction. The Bible gives you clear-cut guidelines on how to recognize deception and keep free from all forms of spiritual blindness. Deception, Delusion & Destruction unmasks deception, reveals its most likely targets, and explains how you can recognize it in its most deadly form — religious deception.

0-938020-43-9 .... $4.95

FAITHBUILDING VIDEO MESSAGES VHS
by Dave Williams

PACESETTING LEADERSHIP

Pastor Dave's highly acclaimed "Pacesetting Leadership" class on video. Topics include: Levels of Leadership, Qualities Exhibited in Master-Level Leaders, The Kind of Leader God is Looking For, How to Overcome Stress and Pressure in the Ministry, and *so much more.*

14 Sessions $239.70

MINISTRY GROWTH AND SUCCESS

Dave Williams' Advanced Leadership Course on video. You'll learn: How to Lead So People See It's God • How to Minister the Holy Spirit Baptism • Church Diseases & Cures • How to Motivate People • Getting Things Done • Writing as a Ministry

10 Sessions $171.25

WHAT TO DO WHEN YOU'VE LOST YOUR MOTIVATION

• The Importance of Motivation • What Happens When We Lose Our Motivation • What Causes a Loss of Motivation • How To Revive Your Motivation

2 Hour Video $19.95

• Quantity Discounts Available •
MOUNT HOPE PUBLICATIONS
202 S. Creyts Rd. • Lansing, MI 48917

FAITHBUILDING VIDEO MESSAGES
VHS by Dave Williams

THE PASTOR'S PAY

A motivational one-hour video featuring Dave Williams speaking about the minister's pay. This video will motivate pastors and board members to study, in depth, how God feels about the pastor's pay.

1 Hour Video $12.95

THE UNPARDONABLE SIN AND THE SIN UNTO DEATH

- Confusion Over the "Unpardonable Sin" • How Can We Understand the Unpardonable Sin • 5 Phases to Committing the Unpardonable Sin • 2 Types of Death • 3 Keys to a Longer Life • Some Who Came Under the Sin Unto Death • Some Who Repented in Time

2 Hour Video $19.95

YOUR GREATEST WEAPON IN THE STORMS OF LIFE

- A Great Lesson In Faith • The Power of Life is in the Tongue • The Kind of Words Jesus Spoke • How to Speak the Results You Want • Faith Words — Your Greatest Weapon Against the Storms of Life

2 Hour Video $19.95

10 COMMANDMENTS FOR GUARANTEED FAILURE

- Success or Failure . . . The Choice Is Yours
- 10 Commandments Guaranteed to Make You a Successful Failure . . . OR
- Don't Do These and You'll Succeed

1 Hour Video $12.95

For your convenience, you may order any product listed here by using the form on the following pages.

• Quantity Discounts Available •
MOUNT HOPE PUBLICATIONS
202 S. Creyts Rd. • Lansing, MI 48917

FAITHBUILDING PRODUCTS
for Pacesetting People by Dave Williams

ORDER FORM

Qty.	Title	Price	Amt.

BOOKS

Qty.	Title	Price	Amt.
___	The A.I.D.S. Plague	1.95	_____
___	Deception, Delusion & Destruction	4.95	_____
___	Supernatural Soulwinning	1.95	_____
___	Somebody Out There Needs You!	1.75	_____
___	End Time Bible Prophecy (Study Notes)	1.75	_____
___	Supernatural Gifts of the Holy Spirit (Study Notes)	1.75	_____
___	The Secret of Power With God	2.95	_____
___	The Christian Job-Hunter's Handbook	3.25	_____
___	The NEW LIFE: The Start of Something Wonderful	1.95	_____
___	The NEW LIFE (Spanish Edition)	1.95	_____
___	Setting & Reaching Your Faith Goals	3.95	_____
___	Genuine Prosperity: A Biblical Perspective	1.25	_____
___	How to Get Out of the Tormenting Cave of Depression	1.50	_____
___	Growing Up in Our Father's Family	1.25	_____
___	You Can Win With Patient Determination (microbook)	1.00	_____
___	The Beauty of Holiness	1.25	_____
___	The Grand Finale: A Study on the Coming End-Time Revival	1.75	_____
___	The Ministry of the Laying On of Hands	1.75	_____
___	Lonely in the Midst of a Crowd	1.25	_____
___	Understanding Spiritual Gifts	1.75	_____
___	The Desires of Your Heart Can Become Realities	2.95	_____
___	Remedy for Worry & Tension	1.25	_____
___	7 Signposts on the Road to Spiritual Maturity	1.50	_____
___	Getting to Know Your Heavenly Father	1.50	_____
___	Revival Power of Music (microbook)	1.00	_____
___	Slain in the Spirit: Is It Real or Fake?	1.50	_____
___	Finding Your Ministry & Gifts	5.95	_____
___	The Art of Pacesetting Leadership	7.95	_____
___	The Pastor's Pay	4.95	_____
___	Tongues and Interpretation (microbook)	1.00	_____
___	15 Big Causes of Failure (microbook)	1.00	_____
___	How to Invest An Hour in Prayer	1.75	_____
___	Success Principles from the Lips of Jesus	2.95	_____

COURSES

Qty.	Title	Price	Amt.
___	The Art of Pacesetting Leadership	69.95	_____
___	Ministry Growth & Development	59.95	_____
___	Your Financial Success	37.95	_____
___	Supernatural Gifts of the Spirit	37.95	_____
___	Successful Church Governments	59.95	_____

AUDIO CASSETTE SETS

___ The Pastor's Pay (2 cassettes)	10.00 _____
___ Relief from Worry & Pressures (3 cassettes)	15.00 _____
___ Spiritual Warfare (12 cassettes)	50.00 _____
___ Fasting for the Impossible (2 cassettes)	10.00 _____
___ The Coming "Grand Finale" Revival (4 cassettes)	20.00 _____
___ The Supernatural Gifts (4 cassettes)	20.00 _____
___ Your Greatest Weapons in the Storms of Life (2 cassettes)	10.00 _____
___ Intercessory Prayer (3 cassettes)	15.00 _____
___ What To Do When You've Lost Your Motivation (2 csts)	10.00 _____
___ End-Times Bible Prophecy (3 cassettes)	15.00 _____

VIDEOS

___ 10 Commandments for Failure	12.95 _____
___ Your Greatest Weapon in the Storms of Life	19.95 _____
___ What To Do When You've Lost Your Motivation	19.95 _____
___ The Art of Pacesetting Leadership (14 sessions)	239.70 _____
___ Ministry Growth & Development (10 sessions)	171.25 _____
___ The Pastor's Pay (1 session)	12.95 _____

TOTAL ORDER $ _____

Please include Payment with Order. Thank You!

DISCOUNT & QUANTITY PRICES: Discount and quantity prices are available for ministers, churches, non-profit organizations, and book stores. Please write to DAVCO COMMUNICATIONS, P.O. Box 80386, Lansing, MI 48917-0386 or telephone (517) 321-2780.

INDIVIDUAL ORDERS: For individual orders, please write to: THE HOPE STORE, 202 S. Creyts Road, Lansing, MI 48917. Tel: (517) 321-2780

Michigan Residents: Please include appropriate sales tax.

Orders are processed immediately upon receipt. Please include full payment with your order. It helps us to serve you better, avoiding C.O.D.s and billings. VISA and MasterCard orders accepted.

PLEASE PRINT CLEARLY

Name _____

Address _____

City _____

State _____ ZIP _____

Please include $1.50 for postage and handling on all orders less than $20.00. Thanks!

VISA _____ MasterCard _____

Expiration Date _____

Signature _____